The Criminal Court: How It Works

Roberta Rovner-Pieczenik
Police Foundation

Lexington Books
D. C. Heath and Company
Lexington, Massachusetts
Toronto

Library of Congress Cataloging in Publication Data

Rovner-Pieczenik, Roberta.
  The criminal court.

  Includes index.
  1. Criminal justice, Administration of—United States. 2. Criminal
courts—United States. 3. Judicial process—United States. I. Title.
KF9223.R69   345'.73'01   76-42854
ISBN 0-669-01056-1

Copyright © 1978 by D.C. Heath and Company.

Published simultaneously in Canada.

Printed in the United States of America.

International Standard Book Number: 0-669-01056-1

Library of Congress Catalog Card Number: 76-42854

The Criminal Court:
How It Works

To my husband, Steve, who lived this book with me and loved me in spite of it.

Contents

42096

List of Figures

List of Tables

Preface

This volume was written to offer a new way of looking at an old institution. In it I try to convince the reader that the criminal court can be viewed as a large-scale organization, and that some of the same approaches that are used to understand hospitals and schools are appropriate to explain the adjudication and sentencing of felony cases processed in the criminal courts. For this purpose I present three models that give meaning to different sets of court-produced data and which should be used in a complementary fashion to more fully explain the courts. Institutional goals, subgroup needs and individual concerns provide the dynamics of court operation—the Rational Actor Model, the Organizational Process Model and the Bureaucratic Politics Model provide the accompanying theoretical bases. Although the data used for analysis is from 1967, it is not dated. Unfortunately, the court studied, and numerous others throughout the country, have not changed enough to significantly alter the conclusions reached or interpretations given.

I owe a great debt to an individual whom I have yet to meet and personally thank. In *Essence of Decision: Explaining the Cuban Missile Crisis,* Graham Allison sorted out an overwhelming amount of data, giving it the order, meaning and clarity which only a fine analytic mind can do. The three models discussed in this book were used by Allison to explain the missile crisis, and his interpretation of these models has been used to analyze the court crisis.

I would also like to thank two very different groups of individuals for aiding me in bringing this volume into existence. The first group helped a treatise in search of acceptance as a doctoral dissertation. Richard Quinney, my academic advisor, was largely responsible for my interest in criminology by giving life to theory and enjoyment to my years of graduate education. Elliott Golden, my mentor in the "field," introduced me to the real world of criminal justice and injustice and allowed me to have a research experience that I will always remember. M. Pat Golden and Larry Seigal, friends and colleagues, were helpful in the final draft of the dissertation and participated in the emotions of "defense day."

The second group of friends and colleagues provided me with the kind of critical comments that enabled my research to become a book. For this I owe thanks to John Greacen, Vera Newman, Martha Lane, Lou Riccio, and Neil Bomberg.

My unending gratitude, however, goes to my husband, Dr. Steve R. Pieczenik. Not only did he expand my sociological perspective by introducing me to his world of political science and international affairs, but also for a period of time too long to ever forget he was a source of support, encouragement and confidence.

The Criminal Court:
How It Works

1 The Criminal Court in Perspective

It is difficult to pinpoint exactly when or why the criminal courts in Metrocourt[1] stopped working in the way the Constitution promised. By 1936, in response to criticism of court practices, Metrocourt's state legislature attempted to curtail the discretionary powers of the prosecuting attorney by requiring a submission to the court, in writing, of a statement of reasons when recommending the acceptance of a particular plea.[2] In 1942 two social scientists teaching in the city served by Metrocourt pointed out that political scientists, reformers, and "politicians out of power" viewed the widespread practice of accepting a guilty plea with alarm.[3] In 1951 a local practicing attorney noted that the major contributor to injustice in the courts was the process through which large numbers of felony cases were eliminated through pleas of guilty to a lesser offense.[4] Approximately six years prior to this study Metrocourt, in the name of modernization and simplification, underwent its first reorganization in 115 years. Critics of the old system had attacked it as an antiquated, inefficient hodgepodge of courts. They charged it with overlapping jurisdictions, waste and confusion, unnecessary congestion and delay in the trial of cases, and undue expense and hardship to people who become enmeshed in legal troubles. The reorganization of Metrocourt resulted in the abolition of old courts, the mergers of others, and the establishment of new court sections.

What, then, characterizes the "new" Metrocourt? The following statements are conclusions which have been generalized from the data gathered and analyzed in this volume. First, the criminal trial, of great theoretical and practical significance to the development of this country's legal system, has been surpassed as the most common method of adjudicating defendants. Second, while the criminal code governing Metrocourt exists to declare what conduct is criminal and prescribe the punishment to be imposed for such conduct, informal understandings among legal officials create a shadow code which guides everyday court operations. Third, the legal evidence brought to bear on a case may have less of a relationship to case disposition (i.e., final charge) than do the characteristics of those attorneys who present and argue such evidence before the court. The chapters which follow intend to support these conclusions with data and rationale.

Three Models of Adjudication

Can conclusions about the daily operations of the criminal courts be understood within a theoretical context? It is the premise of this volume that the use of

1

models are particularly helpful. The use of models in analyzing any complex social system serves a variety of purposes. Models supply a guide for analysis. They lead an investigator to the exploration of postulates and assumptions which underlie analysis. They sensitize the researcher to the larger implications of his/her analysis.[5] According to Kuhn, some models are more successful than their competitiors in solving problems that concern the researcher; these models usually remain in use until a more explanatory one is uncovered.[6]

How does the criminal court function to adjudicate felony cases? This basic question can lead to an exploration of a variety of models for exactness of "fit," each concerned with explaining some aspect of organizational behavior. It is typical for researchers to select one model, or one perspective, from which to view the data and insights produced in the course of a study. This volume differs in that not one, but *three models which describe the behavior of large-scale organizations have been selected to help understand the criminal courts.* The models used in the following chapters have not been created for this volume. The author has, rather, selected existing models which perform well in explaining some aspect of court behavior.

The three models offer differing perspectives on adjudication in the criminal courts.[7] These models—the Rational Actor, Organizational Process, and Bureaucratic Politics models—are complementary. Each model distinguishes different features of court operations as relevant in the overall understanding of felony adjudication. Taken together they highlight different levels of court functioning. It will be apparent in the following sections and later discussions that each model magnifies one set of factors over another and adds a dimension which, when considered complementary, performs well in the analysis of felony adjudication in Metrocourt.

The Rational Actor Model

Most criminal-court analysts explain and predict the behavior of the criminal court in terms of the rational actor, or "classical" model. In spite of innumerable operational complexities and disparate information, these analysts attempt to understand what happens in the criminal court as the more or less purposeful acts of the court as a unified entity. The criminal court is personified as a Rational Actor which selects and chooses.

The Rational Actor Model, in general, attempts to explain action by looking at an organization's objectives. This model assumes that: (a) an action occurs which must be explained; (b) the action reflects purpose or intent; (c) the actor is a collective which acts as one; and (d) the action chosen is a calculated solution to an operational problem. Thus, the explanation consists of exposing what objective(s) the organization is pursuing when it acts, and demonstrating how its actions are reasonable, given the objective. Rationality, according to this model, is equated with making "optimum choices"; that is, in selecting the most efficient alternative, the alternative that maximizes output for a given input. The model further assumes that the actor, the unified entity, is aware of the alternatives available and likely consequences of each alternative. Rational action, then, is selecting an alternative whose consequences are preferred because of their utility.[8] Predictions about what a court might do are based upon calculating the rational thing to do in a given situation, given specific objectives. This approach to understanding organizational behavior is consistent with both classical economic theory and modern game theory.

When applied to the court, the entire process of court adjudication is viewed as one which seeks operationally relevant solutions for the daily problems of court functioning. Just as the police are neither equipped to, nor desirous of arresting each suspected deviant, the courts are neither equipped to, nor desirous of, adjudicating each case arraigned. In a context of a high caseload/low resource imbalance, a relatively typical occurrence in most urban courts, efficiency in the case-flow process can be viewed as the court's main objective. The sieve effect of case screening and most courts' dependence on the guilty plea are processes readily explained through this model. Both are techniques of case-flow management to ameliorate the volume/resource imbalance: they speed adjudication, limit the likelihood of case appeal, make case-flow management flexible, and demand less rigor from legal officials in terms of manpower hours and effort.

The Organizational Process Model

While the Rational Actor Model is helpful in understanding the court's screening behavior, it is not helpful in explaining case dispositions (i.e., actual conviction or plea) and sentencing statistics. Reaching decisions in court—especially through the plea—involves decisions made by two or three subgroup representatives (i.e., prosecution, defense, bench). Disposition and sentencing statistics might best be understood as reflecting internal organizational processes and decision-making dynamics which the prosecutor, defense attorney, and judge play out in court. Such internal dynamics are overlooked by the Rational Actor Model, which reduces these complexities to the behavior of a single actor with a single motive for choice of action. For many purposes, court behavior can be usefully viewed in that manner. However, the Rational Actor Model conceals the fact that organizations, including the court, define alternatives and estimate consequences on the bases of the interests, needs, and perceptions of differing component subgroups.

The Organizational Process Model introduces the notion of interacting subgroups with partially divergent interests, viewing organizational behavior as reflecting a "meeting" or consensus of those interests. This model assumes that no internal consensus necessarily exists within an organization at the level of operational goals. However, problems have to be solved, actions have to be taken, and techniques have to be found for selecting operating strategies. In an organization's search to avoid uncertainty in the behavior of its groups' members, and in its search for resolution of competing group interests, it is led to establish procedural and normative routines, often referred to as standard operating procedures. These routines allow an organization to determine its mode of behavior on the basis of previously established procedures, narrow the range of choices for action open to organizational subgroups, and lend a measure of certainty and consistency in present activities and future expectancies. The approach of this model is consistent with other organizational analyses of decision-making.[9] The analyst has explained the event when the relevant organizational patterns of behavior from which the action emerged have been identified. Predictions tend to identify actions that reflect established organizations and their fixed procedures and programs.

When applied to the court, it is assumed that each legal subgroup—prosecution, defense, bench—works within its own set of interests and constraints, but that their functional interdependence, their operational needs, and their daily interactions promote the emergence of consensus: consensus on how to adjudicate cases and consensus on what cases are "worth." In other words, the institutionalized common orientation that Sudnow observed between the public defender and the prosecuting attorney,[10] and the informal agreements reached between all concerned parties which Blumberg highlights,[11] are the operationalized equivalents of this model's concept of the standard operating procedure or the negotiated work environment.

The Bureaucratic Politics Model

It is easy to see how the Organizational Process Model's view of court behavior as the product of partially coordinated subgroup concerns provides a differing perspective on the court than is found in the Rational Actor's view of court behavior as a choice of a unitary decision-maker for a desired objective. However, the third model, the Bureaucratic Politics Model, looks more closely at individuals within each subgroup as actors in their own right. Actions that are taken and decisions that are made are viewed by this model as political resultants:[12]

... resultants in the sense that what happens ... results from compromise, conflict and confusion of officials with diverse interests and unequal influence; political in the sense that the activity from which decisions and actions emerge is best characterized as bargaining along regularized channels among individual members. . . .

The concept of power plays an important role in this model, viewed as an "elusive blend" of bargaining advantages, skill and will in using bargaining advantages, and other players' perceptions of the first two ingredients. The model further assumes that diverse demands placed on different groups shape their priorities and resulting actions. Conflict is resolved through the use of accrued power.

What happens is a resultant of various bargaining games among players. The event is "explained" by the analyst when s/he has discovered "who did what to whom." Predictions are generated by identifying the fame in which an issue will arise, who the relevant players will be, and their relative power and skill.

Applied to the criminal court—taking the defense attorney as one possible example—this model is alerted to the fact that different attorney groups, specifically, the private and public defenders,[13] are "shaped" differently. Conditions of work (within a bureaucracy or in solo practice), manner of payment (salary or fee), or standards by which each is judged successful (administrative efficiency or a client "hitting the streets") should result in and explain differences in case management and outcome. The need of each attorney subgroup to accrue power and the ability of each attorney to use power differ. Although some studies have reported similar dispositions for the clients of the public and private defender, others suggest a power differential between attorney groups.

Organizational Studies and the Criminal Court

At the beginning of this chapter it was stated that the changes which Metrocourt has undergone can be understood if the court, itself, is viewed as a large organization attempting to harness its resources to achieve its objective; that is, case adjudication. If this picture is accurate, insights from studies of large organizations might be helpful in understanding the criminal court. The following sections are offered to provide the reader with knowledge of the ideas and studies which allow the court to be placed in an organizational perspective.

Organizational Studies in General

Social organization can be characterized by a network of social relations and shared orientations. The former emphasizes the status structure which is defined by relationships, while the latter includes the entire system of shared beliefs which serve as standards for conduct. These dimensions, when deliberately established for purposes of pursuing and achieving goals, constitute the formal aspects of social organization, or the formal organization. The definition of formal organization we will employ in the following chapters is the pattern of division of tasks and power among organizational positions and the rules expected to guide the behavior of the participants.[14]

When in the course of organizational operations practices, values, norms, and social relations arise which have no determinants directly in the official or formal plan, an informal organization has become operational. Blau and Scott have observed that the informal organization is rooted in and nurtured by the formal organization and its arrangements;[15] the informal organization consists of patterns which evolve within the framework of the formally established organization and is comprised of behaviors, norms, and relationships which are dependent upon the formal. It is difficult to understand the operation of the informal system without being concerned with the formal. Suffet, in a study of bail practices in the criminal court, noted that formal bail requirements were necessarily studied in order to identify the variance in standards utilized by court agents.[16]

Early organizational studies were concerned with the formal organization. The "classical school," was concerned with working out the organizational structure which would maximize efficiency and performance. In the classical tradition, concepts of accountability, expertness, conflict settlement, and goal activity were important. Questions concerning the effect of centralization on the efficiency and effectiveness of organizational output were being asked by this group in the early twentieth century.

In reaction to both the formal emphasis and unanticipated consequences of these early studies, the informal aspects of organizational life were uncovered and heralded by the "human relations school." A series of studies undertaken between 1927 and 1932 at the Western Electric Company's Hawthorne works in Chicago demonstrated the power of the small group operating within the confines of the formal system to produce changes in the behavior of individuals.[17] The now famous Hawthorne experiments revealed that: (1) social norms set production levels (in contrast to levels being set by physiological capacities); (2) noneconomic rewards and sanctions affected worker behavior (in contrast to economic-incentive plans); (3) workers acted and reacted as members of a group (and not as individuals); and (4) informal leadership emerged to influence productive behavior (in contrast to the formal organizational positions of authority). From observations such as these the concept of the "informal organization" developed. This particular concept will be important in later chapters of this volume.

It remained for a third development in organizational thought to interphase the two concepts of formal and informal organization. Researchers in the "structuralist school" related both the formal and informal elements of an organization, and extended their investigations to the interplay between the environment and the organization. Government agencies,[18] hospitals,[19] and prisons[20] were a few of the settings which were studied by this group. Abraham Blumberg, applying this perspective to a study of the adult criminal court, outlined the structural relationship of the police, district attorney, judge, accused, and other groups relevant to the adjudication of a felon, paying special attention to some of the internal and external pressures each group exerts and bears in carrying out its function.[21] Emerson, in a study of the juvenile court, focused upon the nature of the court's relations with various organizations and groups within its working environment, and the consequences of these relations for internal operations.[22] In the course of these and other organizational studies, the unofficial (informal) aspects of organizational operations were again raised to the level of visibility.

Criminal Court Organizational Studies

The adult criminal court as a large-scale organization has been the focus of a number of studies over the last decade. However, no comprehensive or unified view of the court has emerged; individual researchers have addressed themselves to different issues for differing reasons. For example, the Rand Institute's study of the New York City criminal court consists of the construction of elaborate flowcharts which describe the flow of defendants through the court, facilitating the identification of operating (structural) problems in the court so that changes in resource allocation could be introduced.[23] No attention, however, is paid to roles, informal norms of substance or procedure, or their relationship to larger organizational concerns. A study of the quality of justice in the lower courts of metropolitan Boston analyzes court process from a case's initial appearance in court through sentencing.[24] While the study details the process of adjudication and specific court problems (e.g., the assignment of counsel), the study does not consistently develop or utilize a theoretical framework through which findings are interpreted.

Other court studies with an organizational purview are limited in the organizational analysis they provide when interpreting data, and the scope of the questions with which they are concerned. One observation study of a lower criminal court was concerned with case dispositions as they related to apprising defendants of their legal rights (i.e., when such an apprisal is done, how it is done, by whom it is done), although reference is made to the court's informal organization and an attorney's ability to enter into "organizational battles irrelevant to the legal status of his case.[25] No attention, however, is paid to distinct levels of organizational operations or the interdependence necessary in case adjudication. Cole's study of the decision to prosecute is concerned with exchange behavior, one concern of the present study, but discusses inter-organizational relationships (among the police, courts, defense attorneys, and community influentials) on the basis of limited, largely exploratory, data.[26]

Sudnow's study of the public defender is focused on the manner in which defendants are represented by the public defender, that is, the "actual" way the penal code is employed in the daily activities of legal representation.[27] The informal norms utilized by public defenders in assessing case seriousness, however, are just one level of analysis found to be pertinent when looking at case adjudication in an organizational framework. Alschuler looks primarily at the plea-bargaining process from the prosecutor's perspective, although his research did not bring him into court, but depended entirely on interview material.[28]

This study was greatly aided by the approach of Abraham Blumberg's *Criminal Justice.*[29] Blumberg, viewing the criminal court as a closed community which has an "almost pathological distrust of outsiders," utilizes twenty years of experience as a lawyer, in addition to years of systematically recording observations and interview material and reviewing psychiatric and probation-department reports as a student of sociology, in an attempt to examine some of the traditional assumptions and ideals of the American legal system as embodied in the criminal court. Many of the conclusions reached by Blumberg are supported in this volume (e.g., institutionalized evasions of due process). However, an attempt has also been made in this study to consider some questions which require statistical information not available to Blumberg. At present, there exists a dearth of adequate empirical research on the effectiveness of defense-attorney representation, for either case dispositions or sentences. This study should increase the factual basis for those arguments which speculate about the relative effectiveness of public-defender representation as compared with representation by the privately retained attorney. In addition, other questions are asked in this volume which were of little concern to Blumberg (e.g., what "rules" comprise the informal normative system of case adjudication, or how are legal officials socialized to have similar interests, given the adversary nature of the criminal court?).

The Vera Institute of Justice study of the prosecution and disposition of felony arrest in the New York City courts offers a particularly interesting comparison to some data presented in this volume. For example, the courts studied were quite comparable to Metrocourt in size, problems, and cases requiring disposition. The techniques of data gathering, depending heavily on case records and interviews, mirrored this study's methodology. The topic itself is almost identical. The Vera study describes the fall-out of felony cases as they make their way through the court system and explores some variables which explain how and why the fall-out takes place.

The perspective used to analyze data, however, and the choice of variables used to explain court behavior are what best distinguish the two works. The Vera study focuses on case fact patterns, the detailed circumstances of the incident, and available legal evidence. The study concludes that, in general, the dispositions were proportional to the seriousness of the offenses, the length of the defendant's criminal record, and the closeness of the defendant's relationship to the victim. The assumption which underlies the analysis, but which is not surfaced, is that made by the Rational Actor Model—that the court responds to the criminal as a monolithic entity. Given this approach, the important ways in which the system's decision-making trip—defender, prosecutor, judge—deal with organizational, subgroup, and personal problems are not explored.[30]

Perhaps the most distinguishing aspect between this work and all others is the application of distinct analytic models—the Rational Actor Model, Organizational Process Model, and Bureaucratic Politics Model—to understand the daily operations of the criminal court. As one complex social system, the court shares with all other social systems a structure comprised of a network of subsystems— each of which can be understood through a variety of perspectives and models. The use of these models highlights the importance of the multiplicity of levels and perspectives which are appropriate for viewing and understanding the criminal court and its officials. They help court analysts avoid the parochialism inherent in viewing court operations from only one perspective and avoid the presentation of data without a theoretical framework for understanding.

Study Methodology

This study was conducted in one criminal court in an eastern city, representative of many of large size and limited resources. A period of observation of the court in question preceded interviews with attorneys and judges, and a subsequent sampling of closed case files. The year focused on was 1967; the issues explored in this volume are as current today as they were then.

The case data on which the statistical analysis of the present study is based were taken from a randomly selected sample of closed criminal-court cases. Two criteria for case inclusion were established: (1) the case must have come to the court's attention charged as a felony, and (2) reached final adjudication during 1967.

The random sample of case files was taken from the records kept by the office of the prosecuting attorney serving Metrocourt and from the clerks' office of the Lower and Superior Court. Four separate random samples were taken according to court section in which a case reached final adjudication:[31]

(1) one hundred cases closed in the Lower Court, initially charged with a felony but never reaching Grand Jury presentation (Lower Court I sample);
(2) one hundred cases arraigned in the Lower Court as a felony, sent to the Grand Jury for indictment, and dismissed by the Jury (Grand Jury sample);
(3) one hundred cases arraigned in the Lower Court as a felony, sent to the Grand Jury for indictment, and returned by the Grand Jury to the Lower Court for adjudication (Lower Court II sample); and

(4) two hundred cases arraigned as a felony in the Lower Court, sent to the Grand Jury for indictment, indicted by the Jury, and sent to the Superior Court for final adjudication (Superior Court sample).

The samples included ten offense categories coming to the attention of the court: assault, burglary, criminal possession, drug abuse, fraud, homicide, larceny, possession of a dangerous weapon, robbery, and sex abuse. Since complete defendant and defense-attorney information was available only for cases indicted by the Grand Jury, the methodology applied was deliberately to choose twice the number of cases from the Superior Court files than from the other court files. Use of this technique insured the inclusion of actual felony convictions, whose proportion in terms of total felony arrests is small.

Interwoven throughout the volume is observational information that both supplements and integrates the other data collected. Prior to the collection of the file information, approximately three months were spent observing the work of the attorney in the prosecutor's office in addition to the operations of Metrocourt. Observation in the first month was "shotgun" in its attempt to comprehend everything that took place; later observations focused on plea negotiations. Observation, in one form or another, continued intermittently throughout the entire period of research.

Decisions about which legal personnel to select for interviews were based on insights that individuals might offer in understanding case-file information. Lists of prospective interviewees were drawn up from personal familiarity or from repetitive case-file appearances, and then discussed with the chief assistant prosecuting attorney. Final selections were based on the probability of a candid response and an individual's frequent involvement with the court. Approximately forty formal interviews were undertaken in addition to the numerous informal ones which occurred continuously in hallways, courtrooms, judges' chambers, and the cafeteria. The officials sought out for formal interviews were judges, defense attorneys, and prosecuting attorneys working daily in the system, while anyone was "fair game" for the informal ones (i.e., newspapermen, secretaries).

To a large extent the present study distinguishes itself from prior court research by using observational, interview, and statistical data in a complementary fashion. Using this approach, the adjudication of felonies in one criminal court is not limited by one set of data generated from only one data-gathering technique. Hopefully, the integration of these data creates a dynamic picture of the operations of the criminal court studied.

Overview of Volume

Procedure in the criminal courts around the nation takes many forms, stemming largely from state and city traditions, peculiarities, and needs. Metrocourt, the criminal court under scrutiny, offers no exception. Chapter 2 outlines the formal procedural organization of Metrocourt, setting the stage for the later concern with the court in daily operation and the adjudication of felony cases. Chapter 3, using the Rational Actor Model, provides an explanation for statistical patterns uncovered for the method of adjudication (i.e., plea, trial, dismissal), and stage of case disposition (i.e., Lower Court, Grand Jury, Superior Court) in Metrocourt. Interviews and observational material are interwoven in this and the succeeding chapters. Chapter 4 focuses on the manner in which court subgroups arrive at dispositions and sentences for pending cases. The Organizational Process Model is invoked to explain subgroup behavior and case outcomes, focusing on standard operating procedures and case assessments which evolve over a period of time. Chapter 5 is concerned with the role of the defense attorney in the representation of cases: the attorney's management of cases through the court as well as the attorney's ability to obtain favorable dispositions and sentences for clients. The concluding chapter summarizes the findings of the preceding chapters and discusses their implications for continued court-related research.

Notes

1. Metrocourt is the name given to the court studied. In reality, it is a large city court operating in a state located on the East Coast.

2. R. Weintraub and R. Tough, "Lesser Pleas Considered," *Journal of Criminal Law and Criminology,* Vol. 32, 1942, 506-30.

3. Ibid.

4. Samuel Dash, "Cracks in the Foundation of Criminal Justice," *Northwestern University Law Review,* Vol. 46, 1951, 385-406.

5. Robert Merton, *Social Theory and Social Structure,* London: Free Press of Glencoe, 1957.

6. Thomas S. Kuhn, *The Structure of Scientific Revolutions,* Chicago: University of Chicago Press, 1970.

7. The models used in this volume have been used with extreme success in interpreting the Cuban missile crisis of 1962. See Graham T. Allison, *Essence of Decision* Boston: Little, Brown & Co., 1971.

8. Ibid.

9. Ibid.

10. David Sudnow, "Normal Crimes: Sociological Features of the Penal Code in a Public Defender Office," *Social Problems,* Vol. 12, 1965, 255-76.

11. Abraham Blumberg, *Criminal Justice,* Chicago: Quadrangle Books, 1967.

12. Allison, op. cit. Used by permission.

13. The public defender studied in this volume should be distinguished from the attorney appointed by the judge at public expense. The public

defender is usually a full-time, salaried employee whose only job is the defense of accused indigents. The appointed attorney is a private attorney whose name is taken from a list before the judge as someone who is willing to accept accused indigent defendants at the governing court rate of reimbursement.

14. Amitai Etzioni, *Modern Organizations,* Prentice Hall, Inc.: Englewood Cliffs, New Jersey, 1964.

15. Peter M. Balu and W. Richard Scott, *Formal Organizations: A Comparative Approach,* New York: Chandler Publishing Co., 1962.

16. Frederick Suffet, "Bail Setting: A Study of Courtroom Interaction," *Crime and Delinquency,* October 1966, 318-31.

17. F.J. Roethlisberger and W. Dickson, *Management and the Worker,* Cambridge, Mass.: Harvard University Press, 1939.

18. Peter M. Balu, *Dynamics of Bureaucracy,* Chicago: University of Chicago Press, 1955.

19. Erving Goffman, *Asylums: Essays on the Social Situation of Mental Patients and Other Inmates,* Garden City, New York: Anchor Books, 1961.

20. Gresham M. Sykes, *Society of Captives: A Study of a Maximum Security Prison.* New York: Atheneum, 1965. Donald R. Cressey, *The Prison: Studies in Institutional Change.* New York: Holt, Rinehart and Winston, 1961. Howard W. Polsky, *Cottage Six: The Social System of Delinquent Boys in Residential Treatment.* New York: John Wiley and Sons, Inc., 1962.

21. Blumberg, op. cit.

22. Robert Emerson, *Judging Delinquents.* Chicago: Aldine Publishing Co., 1969.

23. John B. Jennings, *The Flow of Defendants through the New York City Criminal Court in 1967,* New York: Rand Institute, 1970. John B. Jennings, *The Flow of Defendants through the New York City Criminal Court in 1968 and 1969.* New York: Rand Institute, 1971.

24. Stephen R. Bing and S. Stephen Rosenfeld, *The Quality of Justice in the Lower Criminal Courts of Metropolitan Boston.* Boston: Lawyer's Committee for Civil Rights Under Law, 1970.

25. Maureen Mileski, "Courtroom Encounters: An Observation Study of a Lower Criminal Court," *Law and Society,* Vol. 5, May 1971, 473-539.

26. George F. Cole, "The Decision to Prosecute," *Law and Society,* Vol. 4, February 1970, 331-44.

27. David Sudnow, op. cit.

28. Albert W. Alschuler, "The Prosecutor's Role in Plea Bargaining," *University of Chicago Law Review,* Vol. 36, 1968-69, 50-111.

29. Blumberg, op. cit.

30. Vera Institute of Justice, *Felony Arrests: Their Prosecution and Disposition in New York City's Courts.* New York: Vera Institute of Justice, 1977.

31. The number of cases selected were not meant to be proportionate to the actual number of cases reaching each court section.

2

The Formal Structure
of Metrocourt

In order to place later discussions in perspective, the present chapter describes Metrocourt's formal organization and criminal code.

Court Process

Formal organization was previously defined as a pattern or division of tasks and powers among organizational positions which are expected to guide the behavior of participants. The arrangement of court sections (e.g., arraignment, hearing), constitutes the formal procedural flow of cases from arraignment to disposition (Figure 2-1). At each stage of court processing there exist alternative methods of adjudication (e.g., trial by judge, trial by jury, negotiation for plea, dismissal of case), and alternative types of dispositions (e.g., plea to charge, reduction of charge, conviction by jury, acquittal, dismissal). Although most cases begin the process in Lower Court arraignment (cases initiated by the prosecutor may begin at the Grand Jury), few cases reach disposition in the Superior Court.

From Stationhouse to Court

After the decision to arrest has been made by the police officer, the accused is taken to an intake detention facility—usually a police precinct station. Unless there is, upon review by the officer in charge of the precinct, a lack of evidence constituting "reasonable grounds" for arrest, the accused is "booked."[1] Under the principles of custodial police interrogation specified in the Miranda decision of the Supreme Court, the accused must be informed: (1) of his/her constitutional right to remain silent; (2) that any statement s/he makes may be used as evidence against him/her; and (3) that s/he possesses the right to the presence of an attorney during questioning (either self-retained or appointed). The accused may waive those rights, provided s/he does so voluntarily, knowingly and intelligently. Upon such waiver the resulting statements are then considered legal evidence. When an assistant prosecuting attorney goes to the police station to investigate a serious felony offense, the accused is again notified of his/her rights before any statement is taken. If a stationhouse confession is offered in court as evidence against the defendant, a special hearing is routinely called on the admissibility of the confession, and the prosecution has the burden of proof of a legal waiver.

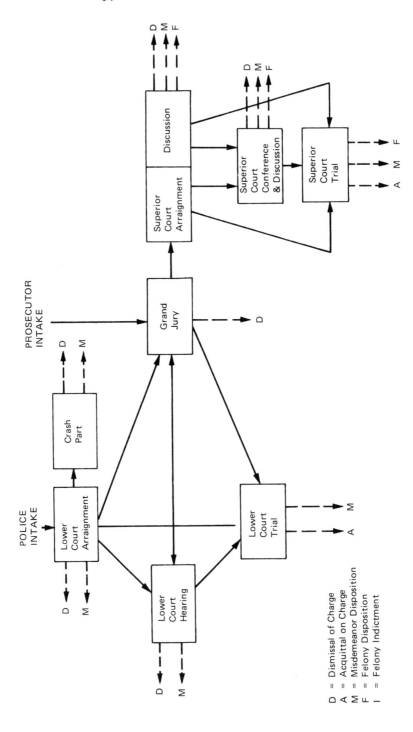

Figure 2-1. Adjudicatory Flowchart for Metrocourt

D = Dismissal of Charge
A = Acquittal on Charge
M = Misdemeanor Disposition
F = Felony Disposition
I = Felony Indictment

After the accused has been booked s/he is fingerprinted (all potential felonies are fingerprintable) and photographed. The accused is then lodged in the lock-up area in the Lower Court while the arresting officer signs a complaint affidavit and receives a docket number for the defendant's arraignment. One copy of the complaint goes to the prosecuting attorney at arraignment.

Case law specifies prompt arraignment after booking. In Metrocourt this usually means an interval of several hours. A writ of *habeas corpus*[2] can be presented to the court challenging the validity of detention, if there is a question of illegal or unlawful detainment.

Lower Court

Arraignment. The purposes of arraignment in the Lower Court are to: (1) publicly state the nature of the charges levied against the individual; (2) determine bail; (3) assign counsel if none has been retained; and (4) set a calendar date for a future court appearance. Both prosecution and defense usually have their first look at the charges filed against the accused, as well as the defendant's record of previous arrests and convictions, only minutes before the case is called before the arraignment bench. The judge quickly appraises the complaint affidavit, the facts of the case as recorded by the arresting officer, the prior arrest-conviction record of the defendant, and a statement made by the defense counsel in behalf of the defendant. At this point, the judge fixes the charge.

The setting of bail involves a discretionary process which is tempered by formal and informal policies of the court. Historically, the system of establishing bail was intended as a device to assure the accused's return to court for further appearance. The law allows judges the discretion to set or deny bail, although according to the Eighth Amendment to the United States Constitution, "Excessive bail shall not be required." In reality, bail-setting becomes for many judges a power with which to punish, to teach the accused a lesson, or to give expression to a personal point of view.[3] One case observed in Metrocourt during the period of study concerned an eighteen-year-old youth residing with his parents, who was given a high cash bail merely to force his parents to come down to court and take an interest in him (as explained by the judge setting bail). The professional literature is replete with instances of misuse of the bail determination.

When a defense attorney makes a special request for bail or makes a motion to reduce it, both the case and amount of bail are discussed, as is the defense's rationale. The role of the prosecutor is to advise the court on bail, although this is done only when the prosecutor disagrees with the sum fixed by the judge. Disagreement is rarely found between judge and prosecutor.

If necessary, court assignment of counsel for the accused is made shortly before the defendant is arraigned. In Metrocourt, public defenders are assigned to all sections of the court. A large majority of all defendants appearing before

Metrocourt are represented by public defenders -the defender office turns down only 15 percent of all those claiming indigency, on the grounds that their income is not below the regulated poverty standard. Usually two attorneys handle a section of the court, so that one is preparing a case while the other is presenting one. The defense attorney who meets his client while the accused is still in the police station is the exception in Metrocourt.

Calendar. After the statement of charge and the fixing of bail, a calendar date is set for the next court appearance. The calendar section of the court is a screening device for cases which are not dismissed or reduced to a misdemeanor during arraignment. Each day hundreds of cases are on the calendar to be sent to hearings, trials, and the Grand Jury. The time between arraignment and hearing (or trial) depends upon court caseload and whether the defendant was unable to make bail or is living in the community.

When the case is called on the calendar the attorney may make an application for adjournment. The attorney will give one of a number of reasons, which the judge may accept or reject. If the application is accepted, a new calendar date for the case is affixed; if rejected, the case will be heard as previously scheduled. Adjournments are often requested when an important witness has not appeared in court or when an attorney is scheduled to appear in another court with another client at the same time. According to one prosecutor, adjournments are frequently used by the defense attorney to manipulate a case in the hope that an extended case will tire the complainant and witnesses with frequent court appearances, and the case will be won by lack of complainant appearance.

Perusal of a typical weekly court calendar revealed that from 80 to 175 new cases and up to 800 old cases are scheduled to be heard in some section of the court. Night court and weekend arraignments add hundreds more cases per week. Exactly 942,693 cases went through the Lower Court in 1967, 17,216 of which were felony arrests.[4]

Hearing. The hearing section of the Lower Court consists of a pretrial examination by a judge who attempts to: (1) establish that a crime, in fact, was committed (*prima facie* evidence[5]); and (2) that there is "reasonable grounds" to believe the defendant committed the crime. Both the defense attorney and defendant are present to question the prosecutor's witnesses, although the burden of proof remains on the prosecution. It is important to understand that each stage of adjudication carries with it a different burden of proof necessary for prosecution. In the hearing stage it is "reasonable grounds"; in the Grand Jury there is an indictment when all legal evidence, taken together, "unexplained and uncontradicted," would be sufficient to warrant a trial; in the felony trial it is whether evidence establishes the defendant's guilt "beyond a reasonable doubt."

The hearing determines whether or not further legal proceedings will be undertaken against the accused, and the nature of these proceedings; it is one of a series of screening stages at which a case can be dismissed, adjudicated, or sent on to the next stage. A decision may be made to reduce the felony charge to a misdemeanor, dismiss it, or present it to the Grand Jury for a felony indictment. Prosecutors agree that many of the reductions which occur at this stage of the proceedings result from insufficient evidence in support of a felony charge. Data for this study reveal that 73 percent of Lower Court I[6] dismissals were due to a withdrawn complaint. This may reflect "overcharging" by the police, be evidence of inefficient police and prosecutorial investigations, or simply a "cooling down" of the complainant. Reductions often reflect standard, informal agreements among court personnel about the seriousness of certain offense categories. Cases which are not reduced or dismissed are sent to the Grand Jury. Some judges, in order to avoid the use of discretion in reductions and dismissals, send every case to the Grand Jury. The prosecutor may encourage this action, not necessarily because of an abundance of evidence, but with the belief that an indictment will give the prosecution a better bargaining position for a felony guilty plea in the Superior Court. On the other hand, one prosecuting attorney commented that the judge who sends every "garbage" case to the Grand Jury is disliked for wasting prosecutorial manpower hours and backlogging the Grand Jury division.

According to Metrocourt felony statistics during the period of study, 27 percent of the "hearing" cases were dismissed, 50 percent were reduced to a misdemeanor and held for Lower Court action, and 23 percent were bound over to the Grand Jury. Of those cases sent to the Grand Jury, approximately 12 percent were dismissed by action of the Jury and 14 percent were returned to the Lower Court as misdemeanor.

Bail may be altered at the hearing. The defense attorney will routinely ask for a reduction of bail if his client is presently in jail, whether or not the reduction will allow his client to be released. This is done for psychological reasons, as well as to place the defendant in a position of being able to make bail the next time a reduction is asked for and given.

As in the arraignment section, the hearing finds the attorneys, papers in hand, taking five minutes to talk in the crowded hallways to complainants and witnesses. Both defense and prosecutorial attorneys try to prepare their witnesses for the questions they will be asked and to anticipate and suggest answers which should be given. In the hearing itself, questioning if often informal, with rules of evidence and procedure not strictly applied.

In establishing a *prima facie* case, the prosecution is often forced to open some of his evidence to the defense. According to one defense attorney, the hearing is often used by the defense as a "fishing expedition" in which he tries to discover the case the prosecution is building and the kind of evidence in his/her possession.

"Crash Part." Because of overcrowded courts and city jails, a "crash part" is periodically instituted in which felony cases are arraigned, reduced (or dismissed), and sentenced during their first court appearance—in return for an immediate plea of guilt. This one-stop adjudication reduces court backlog quickly. According to a public defender involved in this section, dispositions and sentences remain consistent with those typically set when a case goes through the usual court procedure. The defendant, of course, always retains the option of refusing arraignment in this section and going through normal court channels.

According to another public defender, often called upon to represent indigents in this "crash part," the successful operation of this program[7] lies in the working relationship between the judge, prosecuting attorney, and public defender, their similarity in judgment regarding case reductions and their proclivity for such reductions. The periodic introduction of this program in court reflects the presence of a critical management problem and a hoped-for temporary solution.

The Grand Jury

The Grand Jury, or inquest of the people, has come under periodic attack. Ideally, the Jury has as its function the safeguarding of citizens who are being forced to answer felony charges without the state's having satisfied minimum standards of proof. According to its critics, the Jury is little more than the prosecutor's alter ego, or rubber stamp, pretending to be informed and independent, but in fact allowing abuses by the prosecution.[8]

The Grand Jury has the power to indict the accused felon, dismiss the case entirely, or advise the prosecutor to return it to the Lower Court as a misdemeanor (filed as an "information").[9] Its decision is based upon a review of the legal evidence against the accused, presented in closed sessions by the prosecutor. Both defendant and judge are absent from the sessions—although the defendant can ask to appear before the Jury and give evidence on his own behalf. The role of the prosecutor is to present evidence, to instruct the Jury as to the law, and to ask the Jury to apply evidence to law to reach a finding. In addition to his prosecutorial role, the prosecutor is called upon to act in the capacity of judge and defense attorney by insuring that no illegal evidence is presented to the Jury and by respecting the legal rights of the defendant. If the defense attorney believes his/her client's rights have been violated, the attorney proceeds to make a motion to read the minutes of the Grand Jury—which are sealed. If the motion is heard, the minutes of the Grand Jury are read by a judge, who then grants or denies the motion for inspection by the defense attorney.

In Metrocourt, each month begins a new term for each Grand Jury. A Jury consists of twenty-three members. In Metrocourt, eighteen members must be present to conduct court and twelve must be present to indict. Three Grand

Juries usually operate per month, hearing a total of 3,403 cases per year. Within one month, each Jury hears evidence for approximately one hundred cases. If a Jury is dismissed at the end of the month without having taken final action on a case being presented before it, the prosecution must begin case presentation again before the new Jury. Thus, toward the end of each month there is a rush to close all cases, especially cases such as homicide, where a great deal of evidence has been presented and much time has been spent.

Differing court systems operate selectively in their use of the Grand Jury, some districts making more extensive use of them than others. During the period under study, approximately 75 percent of the original felony caseload in the Lower Court of Metrocourt was screened out before reaching the Grand Jury. Jury indictment, however, is needed for a case to be sent to the Superior Court.

Superior Court

Arraignment. After a defendant has been indicted as a felon by the Grand Jury, s/he is arraigned in Superior Court. At this time the charges or "counts" of the indictment are read aloud, bail is set (or reset), and the case is marked for further court action. The defense can then request an immediate conference (the afternoon of the arraignment) if the submission of a guilty plea is being considered, can set a date for the "conference and discussion" section of the court, or reject both options in favor of a jury trial. As in the Lower Court, negotiations are responsible for the adjudication of most cases. The arraignment part of the Superior Court hears approximately twenty-five felony arraignments per day.

Conference and Discussion. The conference and discussion section of the Superior Court serves to legitimize negotiation as a form of adjudication. Prosecutor, defense attorney, and judge discuss each case informally and confer on whether a plea of guilty should be offered or accepted. To capture the format of the session, a simplified version of one conference follows:

Defendant A, female, 36 years old, indicted for Assault I (felony) and Possession of Dangerous Weapon (misdemeanor). During a brawl the defendant shot and wounded the man with whom she had been living out of wedlock. The prosecutor, upon hearing the facts of the case as presented by the defense attorney, offered to accept a plea of guilt to Assault II (a felony). The defense attorney rejoined with an offer of a plea to Assault III (misdemeanor), citing the fact that the defendant had no prior record, a child to support, and should not be imprisoned for this type of crime. The facts of the case were again discussed, this time with the judge asking the defense attorney pointed questions about the defendant. After some three-way discussion and with the prodding of the judge, the prosecution agreed to accept a plea for Assault III and the defense agreed to an "understood" sentence of probation. The defendant was then invited into the room for the first time to tell her story. Before the story ended, the judge, apparently feeling his initial judgment confirmed, stopped the defendant and asked the defense attorney to withdraw his defendant's plea of not guilty and enter a plea of guilty to Assault III to cover all charges. The judge then asked the defendant about her job, education, family, and to repeat her version of the facts of the case, this time "for the record." Before the defendant left the room, the judge informed her she would be returning for sentencing at a later date and that if the probation report had "good things to say" she would not receive a jail sentence.

Many factors were undoubtedly of concern in the above negotiated case: the seriousness of the offense; the likely outcome of the case if it went to trial; the probability of recidivism on the part of the defendant; the possibility of the complaint being withdrawn. The success of the conference and discussion section depends upon a similar assessment of the relevant issues by prosecution, defense, and bench, and the consensus which can be reached by these parties.

It is interesting to note that by this stage of adjudication at least four prosecutors, four defense attorneys (if public defenders), three or more judges, and twenty-three Grand Jurors have heard the case.

Trial. In an adjudicatory system oriented toward negotiations, cases reaching trial may represent failures of the system. In a typical recent year, Metrocourt conducted 245 felony trials, which represented only 10 percent of all cases indicted as felonies. Of these, 53 percent were heard before a jury. In 47 percent of the cases, the defendant waived his/her right to a jury trial and was tried before the court (i.e., before one judge).

Trial by Jury begins with the empaneling of a Jury. Both prosecution and defense are entitled to "cause" and "peremptory" challenges of Jurors.[10] After the Jury is selected, an opening statement is made by the prosecution of what he hopes to prove. An opening statement by the defense attorney is not mandatory. Since there is a presumption of innocence in the law, the defense may choose to hold the prosecution to the burden of proof without making an affirmative defense.

The prosecution presents its case first. Each witness is verbally examined by the prosecutor, who attempts to elicit facts which constitute the crime; this is "direct testimony." Each witness is then subject to "cross examination" by the defense, "redirect examination" by the prosecution (if the defense has elicited new facts, or in an attempt to bolster a weakened witness), and "recross examination" by the defense.

When the prosecution rests its case, a motion is automatically entered by the defense to dismiss the indictment on the grounds that the prosecution has failed to prove a *prima facie* case. If the judge agrees, the trial is over. But if the motion is denied, the judge is in essence saying that s/he believes the elements of crime have been shown and will leave it to the Jury to decide the facts of the case.

A presentation is then made by the defense, in the same manner as that of the prosecution. After this presentation, a motion to acquit is automatically made by the defense, on the grounds that the prosecution has not proven guilt beyond a "reasonable doubt." If this motion is granted, the judge directs the Jury to an acquittal. If not granted, the Jury will be sent to deliberate. The case summation then presented by prosecution and defense is an element of the trial which is particularly dramatic and impassioned.

In order not to oversimplify the trial process, it should be stated that many motions are made for hearings pertaining to matters of evidence and procedure, which serve to prolong the trial process. One hearing considered mandatory for the prosecution occurs when a defendant's confession is offered into evidence. It is at this time that the judge attempts to learn the circumstances under which the confession was made by questioning all involved parties (e.g., defendant, arresting officer). In the long range this may save the court the cost of an appeal after conviction, an appeal on the basis that the confession was in violation of the defendant's Miranda rights and entered into evidence illegally.

Sentencing. Following a guilty plea or verdict, the judge sets a date for sentencing. Depending upon the circumstances of conviction, the judge may consider the advice of the Jury and the court's probation staff. In reality, many judges in Metrocourt will discuss sentence possibilities with the defendant's attorney in order to increase the possibility of a guilty plea. If this is accomplished, the judge informs the defendant of the probable sentence immediately following his/her acceptance of the defendant's plea, barring a presentence report by the probation department which uncovers new information which would warrant a change in the sentence.

This report consists of information on a defendant's prior arrest/conviction record, employment history, family life, educational background, living conditions, and other data which present the life-style of the defendant to the judge. Most judges in Metrocourt stated that the flexibility built into the sentencing code is an important way of individualizing justice. The degree to which this report does, in fact, guide a judge is an individual judge's decision.

According to Metrocourt's Penal Code, sentences for misdemeanor offenses include probation (with and without conditions) and up to one year in the local jail. Sentences for felony offenses include probation and more than one year in the state penitentiary. Although a sentencing range is attached to each charge as noted in the criminal code, each judge has great flexibility in the sentence set for a defendant.

To summarize, the formal adjudication of a felony case through the criminal court entails a procedure involving appearances in many distinct court sections and the daily interaction of many legal agents. The consequences of full adjudication can be elaborate and serious (conviction and sentencing as a felon by a jury trial in the Superior Court) although in reality the majority of cases are either dismissed or pled guilty to a misdemeanor in the Lower Court. Some court sections are overwhelmed with "business," while others remain under-utilized. The procedural complexities appear to become routine as legal agents interact daily and achieve case consensus. The greatest proportion of cases never reach the Superior Court.

The Criminal Code

Enacted statutes identify and codify criminal behavior in Metrocourt. Whether these statutes are the result of the operation of a narrow group of interests or whether they truly represent majority concerns, the criminal code in Metrocourt does establish the boundaries for criminal prosecution and constitutes the basic source of authority, which directs and controls the state's use of the criminal sanction. The many purposes it serves include the following:

1. to proscribe conduct which "unjustifiably and inexcusably" causes or threatens substantial harm to individual or public interests;
2. to give warning of the nature of conduct proscribed and of the sentences authorized upon conviction;
3. to define the act which constitutes each offense; and
4. to differentiate between serious and minor offenses and proscribe proportionate penalties.[11]

Each offense category (e.g., assault, burglary, larceny, robbery) is divided into descriptive subcategories which are ranked according to seriousness of offense (i.e., degrees). Robbery, for example, one of the offenses involving theft, is divided into three degrees: Robbery III is a forcible stealing of property by an offender; Robbery II is a forcible stealing of property by an offender when s/he is aided by another person actually present; Robbery I is a forcible stealing of property by an offender in which in the course of committing the crime or immediate flight therefrom, s/he or another participant in the crime causes serious physical injury to a person not a participant, or is armed with, uses, or threatens to use a dangerous instrument. The offense of Assault, one of the offenses against the person which involves personal injury, is also divided into three degrees.

What is most significant about the criminal code for this study is the distinction which is made between offenses classified as felonies and those classified as misdemeanors. The *felony* is an offense for which a sentence in excess of one year in prison is authorized; the *misdemeanor* is an offense for which a sentence in excess of one year in prison cannot be imposed. The charge of assault, for example, is divided into three degrees, one of which is classified as a misdemeanor. Assault III is a misdemeanor and is defined as follows in Metrocourt's Penal Law:

1. with intent to cause physical injury to another person causes such injury to person or another; or
2. recklessly causes physical injury to another; or
3. with criminal negligence causes physical injury by means of a deadly weapon or dangerous instrument.

Assault II is a felony and is defined as follows:

1. with intent to cause serious physical injury to a person, causes such injury to such person or another; or
2. with intent to cause physical injury to a person, causes such injury to such persons by means of a deadly weapon or dangerous instrument; or
3. with intent to prevent a peace officer from performing a lawful duty, causes physical injury to such peace officer; or
4. recklessly causes serious physical injury to another person by means of a deadly weapon or dangerous instrument; or
5. unlawfully and without consent, gives a drug to another to intentionally cause stupor, unconsciousness or other physical impairment; or
6. in the course of an in furtherance of the commission or attempted commission of a felony, other than a felony in the article of sex offenses, or of immediate flight therefrom, he, or another participant causes physical injury to a person other than one of the participants.

It is important to highlight the consequences flowing from the label that is eventually applied to the specific act: Assault III is a misdemeanor and brings with it a potential prison sentence of up to one year and/or probation, or a suspended sentence; Assault II carries a potential maximum sentence of seven years in prison, without provisions for either probation or suspended sentence. As a misdemeanor, an Assault III sentence is served in the local jail (or "workhouse," as it is called by Metrocourt) while as a felony, an Assault II sentence is served in a state penitentiary.

Bearing in mind the importance of the felony-misdemeanor distinction, the ambiguity of language found in the criminal code and the flexibility it allows in applying code language to a specific act should be noted. For example, terms such as "physical injury" and "serious physical injury" can distinguish between the felony and misdemeanor (as above) and are defined in the code as follows:

"Physical injury" means impairment of physical condition or substantial pain.
   "Serious physical injury" means that which creates a substantial risk of death or which causes death or causes serious and lengthy disfigurement or lengthy impairment of health or loss or impairment of bodily function.

Thus, deciding upon the nature of intended pain (i.e., "substantial" rather than "serious" and lengthy impairment to health) becomes one judgmental issue upon which discretion must be exercised.

Another example: the term "intent" is particularly troublesome, due to the confusion that surrounds that term and other culpable states required for particular crimes. Under the criminal code of Metrocourt, Criminal Trespass I (a misdemeanor) is distinguishable in description of offense from Burglary II (a felony carrying a maximum sentence of seven years) only by the phrase "intent to commit a crime therein." This distinction, and others made in the criminal code between the culpable mental states of "intentionally," and "knowingly" or "recklessly" and "negligently," are open to interpretation.

Since the overwhelming majority of criminal-court cases are decided without recourse to trial, but by the plea of guilty, the daily interpretations of prosecutors, defense attorneys, and judges as to the seriousness of an offense provide the reality to the criminal code's provisions. Notwithstanding the occasional cry that the absence of continuing legislative review of criminal codes results in the "perpetuation of anomalies and inadequacies which have complicated the duties of police, prosecutor, and courts and have hindered the attainment of a rational and just penal system,"[12] the application of any criminal code necessitates discretion.

Notes

1. "Booking" is an administrative procedure involving a recording of the description of an offense, facts about the accused (name, address, age), circumstances of the arrest, and the charge.

2. A writ of *habeas corpus* is the name given to a variety of orders from a court to an official to bring the body before the court.

3. Ronald Goldfarb, *Ransom: A Critique of the American Bail System.* New York: John Wiley and Sons, 1965, p. 46.

4. All summary statistics of court cases are from the Annual Report, Indictments and Dispositions, Superior Court and Grand Jury, of the District Attorney's Office under study, 1967.

5. *Prima facie* evidence is such evidence as in the judgment of the law is sufficient to establish a given fact constituting the party's claim and which if not rebutted or contradicted will remain insufficient.

6. Cases reaching final disposition in the Lower Court are referred to as Lower Court I. Those cases which are sent to the Grand Jury for felony indictment but are returned to the Lower Court as a misdemeanor are referred to as Lower Court II.

7. "Success" is measured in this part by the number of cases which are disposed of each day.

8. L.P. Watts, Jr., "Grand Jury: Sleeping Watchdog or Expensive Antique?" *North Carolina Law Review,* 37, April 1959, 290-315. Walton Coates, "Grand Jury, The Prosecutor's Puppet," *Pennsylvania Bar Association Quarterly,*

33, March 1962, 311-17. "Grand Jury, Past and Present: A Survey, *American Criminal Law Quarterly,* 2, Spring 1964, 119-44.

9. The accusation of the Grand Jury is called an "indictment," "bill of indictment," or "true bill." The "information" is another form of accusation, made by the prosecutor to the Lower Court when a Grand Jury indictment is not forthcoming.

10. A challenge for "cause" is a challenge to a juror for which some cause or reason is alleged. A "peremptory" challenge is a challenge which the prosecutor or the defendant is allowed to have against a certain number of jurors without assigning any cause.

11. *Penal Law: A Guide for Police Officers.* Metrocourt: Municipal Police Training Council, 1967.

12. *Task Force Reports: The Courts.* Washington, D.C.: Government Printing Office, 1967.

3 The Rational Decision in Court

To understand the operation of any organization—a hospital, a school, a court—one must consider its goals. Goals, however, come in two varieties: those that are stated and those that are real. Differences between these two sets of goals can be summed up as those which appear on paper and those which absorb the organization's resources and the commitments of its employees. Stated goals, unfortunately, frequently conflict with the "daily running of business." In cases of conflict, the real goals have clear priority.

Organizational activity tends to be molded by actions toward goals which provide operationally relevant solutions for the daily problems of the organization. The daily problems of the court revolve around adjudicating an overwhelming number of cases with limited resources. The court's solution to these problems can be understood by using the Rational Actor Model to interpret daily adjudication decisions.

This chapter outlines the basic assumptions and concepts which underlie the Rational Actor Model. This model is invoked in an attempt to demonstrate its usefulness in making sense out of statistics on (a) method of adjudication (i.e., dismissal, trial by jury, plea of guilt) and (b) the stage of adjudication (i.e., the drop-out of cases at different stages between initial arraignment and final disposition).

The Rational Actor Model

The Rational Actor Model always attempts to explain the actions of an organization by looking at its objectives. RAM starts off by assuming that most actions are deliberate: they are calculated solutions by organizational actors to operations problems. To understand an organization, then, its objectives must be exposed and its actions must be demonstrated to be reasonable in terms of its objectives.

Rationality, in this model, is also equated with making optimum choices, in terms of the efficiency of alternatives selected. This approach goes as follows: in order for any action to maximize output (or "profits") and minimize input (or "costs") the actor must be aware of the alternatives available and the likely consequences of each alternative. Rational action, then, is selecting an alternative whose consequences are preferred because of their utility.[1]

Economists, political scientists, and sociologists have all studied behavior as purposeful, goal-directed activity. Rational action has been treated at length in decision-making and game theory:[2]

Classical "economic man" and the rational man of modern statistical decision theory and game theory make optimal choices in narrowly constrained, neatly defined situations. In these situations rationality refers to an essentially Hobbesian notion of consistent, value-maximizing *reckoning* of adaptation within specified constraints. In economics, to choose rationally is to select the most efficient alternative, that is, the alternative that maximizes output for a given input or minimizes input for a given output. . . . In modern statistical decision theory and game theory, the rational decision problem is reduced to a simple matter of selecting among a set of given alternatives, each of which has a given set of consequences: the agent selects the alternative whose consequences are preferred in terms of the agent's utility function which ranks each set of consequences in order of preference.

In short, rationality refers to consistent, value-maximizing choice within specified constraints.

The basic assumptions and concepts of the Rational Actor Model can take the form of propositions:[3]

1. The *goals and objectives* of the organization are translated into a "payoff" or "utility" or "performance" function which represents the "value" of alternative consequences, stemming from alternative decisions.
2. The rational organization must choose among a set of *alternatives* displayed before it in a particular situation.
3. To each alternative is attached a set of *consequences* or outcomes of choice that will ensue if that particular alternative is chosen.
4. *Rational choice* consists simply of selecting that alternative whose consequences rank highest in the decision-makers' payoff function.

When applied to the court setting, the goals and objectives of the court become *efficiency in case adjudication*. Just as the police are neither equipped to, nor desirous of, making an arrest in all criminal cases, the courts are neither equipped to, nor desirous of, adjudicating each case arraigned. In the context of a high case volume and limited resources, the Rational Actor Model is particularly appropriate for explaining decisions that have to be made to enable the court to function under the volume/resource imbalance.

The model's appropriateness became apparent (i.e., the assertion that administrative efficiency is an operational objective which overrides all other objectives) during a preliminary review of the study's data. In an effort to uncover, through statistics, whether patterns of felony adjudication occur, it was found that (1) case screening occurs at each stage of adjudication, resulting in only 12 percent of all arraigned felonies reaching the superior court for possible felony adjudication, and that (2) cases which are adjudicated guilty in Metrocourt are done so primarily through the mechanism of the guilty plea (rather than the Jury trial). The "whys" of these above statistics were uncovered during interviews and observations and led to a decision about the appropriateness of the RAM. Thus, understanding the importance of administrative efficiency evolved from an attempt to explain statistics.

Why are cases screened out as adjudication continues? To arrive at an answer, alternative reasons should be considered, such as a lack of strong evidence, the decision of a complainant not to prosecute, or the mandatory freedom for defendants' release if cases continue longer than "speedy trial" statutes allow. By examining various aspects of court administration and the concerns of its administrators, one would pick through a variety of potential reasons for "screening out," eliminating some reasons and adding others. Any attempt to explain court events by recounting the concerns and calculations of the court is the trademark of the Rational Actor Model.

This approach is not limited to court analysis. Consider an example from an earlier criminal-justice stage. When confronted with the arrest decision, that is, the decision to take a suspect into custody, Wayne LaFave's major work in this area uncovered a variety of rationale for invoking or not invoking the criminal process.[4] For example, police frequently do *not* invoke the criminal process because (1) the legislature does not desire enforcement; (2) there are limited enforcement resources; (3) the arrest situation is inappropriate; (4) an arrest would cause loss of public respect; (5) failure to arrest would benefit the law-enforcement system; or (6) arrest would cause harm to the offender or victim which would outweigh any risk from inaction. This explanation for not using arrest authority presents a series of arguments that permit interpretation of police behavior as a value-maximizing choice. For each example given the decision not to arrest contains more potential benefits to the police, in either the short-run or long-range, than would the decision to arrest.

In similar fashion, we could question why a prosecutor might decide to accept a plea of guilty to a reduced charge. Donald J. Newman offers various reasons:[5] (1) conviction on the maximum charge is unlikely because of insufficient evidence, reluctant witnesses, or upon the advice of the judge; or (2) a lesser charge is more appropriate to avoid a record of conviction on the original offense (e.g., rape) or to individualize justice. Here again, the method Newman employs in explaining the behavior of prosecution is to construct a rational approach to decision-making.

What is striking about the arrest and prosecution examples is *the similarity in approach which researchers used when called upon to produce explanations.* Each assumed that what must be explained was an action, i.e., behavior reflecting purpose or intention. In each instance, the action was the generalized entity; that is, police in the first instance, prosecution in the latter. Each assumed that the decision was a calculated solution to an important problem. For each, explanation consisted of indicating the goal the actor was pursuing when it acted, and how the action was a reasonable choice given the actor's overriding obligations.

Efficiency in Adjudication

The major adjudicatory methods in Metrocourt are the dismissal, plea of guilty, and trial by jury.[6] According to Table 3-1, indicating method of adjudication by stage of disposition, of those cases arraigned in the Lower Court which do not reach Grand Jury presentation (Lower Court I), 39 percent are dismissed, 51 percent plead guilty, and 10 percent go to trial. Once a case reaches the Superior Court, a dismissal (2 percent) or a trial (6 percent) is unlikely, and the plea of guilt is responsible for 92 percent of the adjudications. Such findings further validate the conclusions of the 1967 President's Commission on Law Enforcement and Administration of Justice that most criminal cases are disposed of outside the traditional trial process[7] and reveal that *the plea of guilty plays a major adjudicatory role at every stage of adjudication in Metrocourt.*

Utility of the Guilty Plea

The functional utility of the plea (vs. the trial) as an adjudicatory mechanism has been commented upon by previous researchers. Questionnaires sent to federal district court judges revealed that the plea is considered an administrative "tool"

Table 3-1
Method of Felony Adjudication by Stage of Adjudication

| | *Sample Statistics, 1967, Metrocourt* | | |
| | | *Stage of Final Adjudication* | |
Percent Method of Adjudication	*Lower Court I*[a]	*Lower Court Return II*[b]	*Superior Court*[c]
Dismissal	39.0	41.2	2.1
Plea	51.0	35.0	91.7
Trial	10.0	23.8	6.2
Total numbers	100	80	192

[a]Arraigned as felonies, reached final adjudication in Lower Court without Grand Jury presentation.

[b]Arraigned as felonies, presented to the Grand Jury for indictment, returned by the Jury to the Lower Court for adjudication.

[c]Arraigned as felonies, presented to and indicted by the Grand Jury as a felony, adjudicated in the Superior Court.

where there is limited staff and budget; the plea helps in the efficient and economical administration of criminal law.[8] It is interesting to note that in 1942 "political scientists, reformers and politicians out of power" were viewing "with alarm the practice of the acceptance of pleas of guilty to a lesser charge. . . ."[9] Another early article on the plea of guilty revealed that the "injustice" of the plea was caused by statistics showing that approximately 32 percent of the cases in one jurisdiction between 1948 and 1950 were pleaded guilty to a lesser offense.[10] Metrocourt's use of—if not dependence upon—the guilty plea underscores the relatively rapid displacement of the trial by the plea, which has taken place over twenty-five years. The following discussion focuses on the rational utility of the plea for the criminal court in terms of: (1) speed of adjudication; (2) ease of operations; (3) limited case return; and (4) flexibility in case management.

Speed of Adjudication. The advantages of a large proportion of case dismissals for minimizing case backlogs are obvious. Less obvious, perhaps, are the advantages of the plea of guilt over the trial mechanism. Metrocourt sample statistics reveal that the time taken by the trial procedure exceeds that of the plea procedure at all stages of adjudication. Cases going to trial in the Lower Court (without Grand Jury presentation) average 7.3 months from initial arraignment to final adjudication, while cases pleaded guilty average 2.2 months; cases returned to the Lower Court by the Grand Jury average 7.5 months and 5.8 months, respectively; cases adjudicated in the Superior Court average 6.9 months and 4.3 months, respectively. Trial time exceeded plea time for every offense category.

Once a case has been presented to the Grand Jury it will be more quickly adjudicated in the Superior Court than when it is returned to the Lower Court. Case backlog differences between courts may account for some of this difference.

According to one public defender, the plea is a "necessary evil" in both courts:

Everyone is entitled to a trial, theoretically. But due to court backlog it's impossible. The backlog (for trial) up here (Superior Court) can be up to 14 months—and that's because 90% of the cases are disposed of without trial. (Public Defender, Superior Court)

Whether or not this attorney's statistics are correct, he (and other court officials) perceive them to be true and justify the plea system on that basis. One judge of the Lower Court put it this way:

All plea bargaining can conceivably take less than a minute or two, even for the most serious crime. . . . The refusal of a reasonable reduction and the loss of the plea will tie up the court for days or weeks. (Judge, Lower Court)

The model timetable for the adjudication of felonies proposed by the 1967 President's Commission suggested that the period from arrest to trial of felony cases be not more than four months.[11] Without the plea mechanism, which presently "allows" felony cases to be tried in seven months or longer, there is little doubt that the time gap would be even greater and that cases would be backlogged for years.

Ease of Operations. Most court officials interviewed expressed the opinion that recent Supreme Court interpretations of the rights accorded individuals charged with felonies have made conviction by trial more difficult to achieve. According to one judge in the Lower Court: "They (the higher courts) have given us a lot of work. A conviction is harder to obtain." Along with the decision to go to trial are necessary decisions on a panoply of potentially time-consuming challenges and hearings. For example, a defendant accused of armed robbery who chooses to stand trial for the offense can insist upon one hearing concerning the admissibility of evidence in court, another on the legality of the police officer's search and seizure, and another on the violation of his rights at the time of accusation. In addition, this defendant can insist upon a hearing on the validity of witness-identification procedures, and on the voluntariness of his confession. Some of these hearings are already standard operating procedure in Metrocourt and are viewed as increasing the uncertainty of conviction by trial.

Accepting pleas of guilty place few, if any, restrictions on what the prosecutor, defense attorney, and judge will consider relevant for discussion. Much of their discussion takes place outside of the presence of the defendant and "off the record." The depth of case investigation and analysis necessary in public adversary proceedings becomes less important in a plea-bargaining procedure. According to Newman in *Conviction,* not only does the guilty plea avoid the time, expense, and effort of the trial, it also avoids most complex corollary issues.[12] In summary, the omission of several adjudicatory pretrial steps most likely eases case adjudication time in court as well as preparatory time for legal officials.

Limited Case Return. The right of appeal dates back to the nineteenth-century writ of error, authorized and issued by circuit-court judges. The process of appeal, however, is often a drawn-out procedure which absorbs time, manpower hours, and resources. Accepting a plea of guilty can be an effective way of discouraging appeals.

In Metrocourt, a judge in a plea section of the court attempts to protect the court from appeal by requesting that the defendant answer a series of questions in the presence of a public stenographer. One judge of the Superior Court, often placed in the "conference and discussion" section because of his ability to resolve the cases before him through the plea, stated:

Everything I do with a defendant I put on the record. I have what I call "the reading of the will." I read to him, one sentence at a time, the questions I would like him to answer. I make it a point not to talk to a defendant, especially if he is alone. We then avoid *corum nobis*[13] remedies. (Judge, Superior Court)

The procedure this judge follows is typical of many judges in Metrocourt. The following are a series of questions typically posed by this judge during the course of a formal plea of guilty:

To the Defendant: Do you understand English? Do you consent to have this in the robing room?
To the Defense Attorney: Do you have an application (plea)? What is it?
To the Prosecuting Attorney: Is that agreeable to the district attorney?
To the Defendant: Do you understand the charge? (Judge explains it if necessary.) Have you discussed it with your lawyer? Do you accept the charge? Did you in fact commit the offense charged? (Reads description of offense.) Do you understand what your sentence might be if no new information is brought forth in the case when sentence is reviewed? (Reads potential sentence.) Do you have questions regarding the plea or punishment?

The stenographer then reads aloud the notes s/he has just taken of the questions and answers which transpired in the previous minutes. This record is entered as legal evidence if the defendant enters an appeal of the conviction. It is particularly significant that the above conversation follows a few minutes of private conversation between the judge, prosecuting attorney, and defense counsel *prior* to the entrance of the defendant into the room, conversations which could best be characterized as negotiations. It is in the few minutes between the private conversation among legal officials and the entrance of the defendant into the robing room that the defense attorney relates to his/her client what the court feels is an acceptable plea and sentence.

In order to make pleas more attractive to all defendants, a recent law in Metrocourt provided for a promise to be made regarding a certificate of release from civil disabilities. Under this law an individual without any prior record would not be restricted civilly because of a conviction through a plea of guilt (e.g., voting rights, civil-service requirements, liquor license).

Legal scholars have been continually concerned with the constitutionality of the plea, the grounds upon which the entered and accepted plea should be allowed to be withdrawn, and the preventive measures the court must take to eliminate cause for complaint after a plea is submitted. Concern has been expressed in the areas of official misconduct (a plea has been obtained by intimidation, a promise of leniency was unfulfilled), and with the defendant's lack of knowledge concerning the meaning of the plea or its consequences (the charge is not understood, the defendant is not represented by counsel, the plea is offered after a lengthy period of time). Preventive measures such as having the court advise the defendant on the nature of the accusation and the consequences of his plea, having counsel present, curtailing promises made, and taking steps to ensure that the plea is voluntary, have been recommended. The American Bar Association has suggested criteria for determining when an injustice in pleading may have been performed:

1. the defendant was denied the effective assistance of counsel guaranteed him by the constitution, statute or rule;
2. the plea was not entered or ratified by the defendant or a person authorized to act in his behalf;
3. the plea was involuntary, or entered without the knowledge of the charge, or that the sentence actually imposed could be imposed;
4. the defendant did not receive the charge or sentence concessions contemplated by the plea agreement and the prosecuting attorney failed to seek or not to oppose these concessions as promised in the plea agreement.[14]

On the basis of these standards, the above example of the procedure the judge follows in Metrocourt appears to ensure a "satisfied" defendant with little reason to attempt to withdraw a plea once entered. While the trend today is toward increased use of appeal of judgments from trials, appeals in plea-negotiated cases in Metrocourt are almost nonexistent. Elaborate, recorded sessions at which pleas are accepted with litanies that cover every potential ground for later attack ensures "better" pleas; that is, pleas which are more "appeal-proof."

Flexibility in Case Management. While trial proceedings are structurally rigid, pleas offer a flexibility in case adjudication more appropriate to changing external conditions; as case arraignments increase and jails become overcrowded, a mechanism is needed to screen cases quickly and with discretion in considering sentencing alternatives.[15]

The "conference and discussion" section of the Superior Court of Metrocourt structures plea-taking into the court organization. Although the Lower Court has no permanent court section for negotiations, perhaps the epitome of the flexibility possible within a formal system is the "crash part" or "blockbusting part" of the Lower Court. This court "part" or section is periodically organized when court traffic becomes unmanageable or when the city jails become overcrowded:

When jails get overcrowded and the Commissioner of Corrections calls up, they put on a block-busting part. It's only effective with complete cooperation. It's difficult; a pressure on everyone. (Judge, Lower Court)

According to one public defender periodically assigned to this section, it is designed to be a "pressure valve to keep the whole god-damn court system from blowing up." A judge, public defender, and prosecuting attorney who can work easily together, and are amenable to taking pleas, comprise the temporary, "crash part." They are generally considered "pros," individuals who can quickly evaluate a case and reach a mutually agreeable decision. When in operation, the group has been known to dispose of 1,300 cases in two months.

Structured Inducements to Plead Guilty

Although the plea of guilty may be prefered by the court because of its operational utility (speed of adjudication, ease in operations, limited case return, flexibility in case management), every defendant accused of an offense cannot be expected to waive his/her constitutional right to a public trial. Also, since not all defendants are guilty, entering a guilty plea would be inconsistent with America's concept of justice.

But the court "runs" on quick case turnover, i.e., the plea. In order to encourage pleas of guilty, the court structures inducements which make this adjudicatory mechanism desirable. Institutionalized inducements to plead guilty in Metrocourt include (1) placing an unwritten sentencing "penalty" on defendants convicted by a trial procedure; (2) providing a range of favorable, known dispositional and sentencing alternatives; (3) counteracting the "overcharge," which the court maintains and legitimizes; and (4) consolidating charges and sentences.

Sentencing Penalty at Trial

One method of limiting the number of individuals preferring the trial procedure to the plea of guilty is through an unwritten sentencing penalty for those defendants convicted by trial. One defense attorney, among others who voiced the same sentiment, admitted that "most judges, if a man goes to trial, will sentence him to a higher sentence than if he pleads guilty; there seems to be a penalty for going to trial." This "higher" sentence is certainly not in excess of the criminal-code stipulations. There is a good chance, however, the tendency will be to sentence nearer to the maximum allowed.

The small number of trial convictions for the offenses sampled in Metrocourt makes it difficult to confirm this statement statistically. Still, a trend exists in the sentencing patterns of the Lower Court for the charge of felonious assault.[16] Approximately 30 percent of each group (plea and trial) received nonconfinement as a sentence, although defendants who entered a plea of guilty received an unconditional discharge (a discharge with no stipulations concerning supervision or behavior) and those who stood trial received probation (which entails reporting to a probation officer, living under restrictions imposed by the probation department, and the chance of revocation). The average sentence length fixed for those entering a plea in the Lower Court and receiving confinement as a sentence was 3.1 months, while for those standing trial it was 4.3 months. There is no reason to believe that only the more serious cases went to trial. It can be speculated that differences in sentencing in the Superior Court level would be greater because of the "higher stakes" involved with a potential felony conviction.

The American Bar Association in its *Standards Relating to Pleas of Guilty* has taken a stand on this issue. They have suggested the following:

> The court should not impose upon a defendant any sentence in excess of that which would be justified by any of the rehabilitative, protective, deterrent or other purpose of the criminal law because the defendant has chosen to prove his guilt at trial rather than to enter a plea of guilty or nolo contendere.[17]

A questionnaire sent to federal district court judges revealed that 87 percent of those responding said they gave the defendant who pleaded guilty a more lenient sentence than the defendant not pleading guilty. The less severe punishment following a guilty plea was explained away by the judge's reaction that a plea is evidence of a repentant attitude (considered an important step in rehabilitation), while in a trial the defendant is probably committing perjury in his defense and is a partner to "dilatory tactics" of his defense counsel.[18] Perhaps most interesting is the presumption of guilt which underlies the judges' responses.

One public defender added a qualification to this sentencing trend, noting that sentencing discrepancies are more likely to occur with defendants who have a prior record: "those (defendants) with a record, if found guilty (by trial) are hung." The resulting irony seems to be that while the trial may be less harmful to the defendant without a record, if such a defendant is induced to plead guilty, the desirability of going to trial in any future case is markedly decreased.

Favorable, Known Alternatives

The plea of guilt brings with it certainty of outcome—in terms of dispositions and sentences. For example:

> *Case 475* involved a defendant who cashed a series of bad checks at banks where he did not have an account. He offered a plea of guilty to Attempted

Grand Larceny II in the Superior Court and received a suspended sentence. The defendant had a long history of passing bad checks.

The penal code in the above case specifies a sentence of up to seven years' confinement for conviction of Grand Larceny II—with conviction on Attempted Grand Larceny II carrying a maximum sentence of up to three and one-half years' confinement.

> *Case 238* involved a "crap game" in which the defendant lost, would not pay, pulled a gun, and shot one of the players. The defendant was charged with Felonious Assault and Possession of A Dangerous Weapon. Conviction on the Assault charge alone brings with it a sentence of up to 15 years' confinement. The defendant at first insisted upon going to trial. He had a prior conviction record of five assault convictions (misdemeanor convictions). He eventually pleaded guilty to Attempted Assault II and received a sentence of up to 2½ years' confinement.

The penal code in the above case specifies confinement of up to seven years for Assault II, and up to three and one-half years for Attempted Assault II.

It should be noted that since adjudication and sentencing are separated for trial purposes, the defendant loses any bargaining power s/he might have in the plea situation, where adjudication and sentencing are arrived at jointly. Although dispositions and sentences that might have resulted from a trial in the above cases are speculative, it appears that defense counsel, with assent of the defendant, is induced to plead by being provided with a known outcome, one that appears favorable, one that is partially under the defendant's control:

> The court's range of pleas are generous. They are tempting gifts even for the innocent. If I think my client can be proved guilty—whether or not he is—I must of necessity accept the offer. (Public Defender, Lower Court)
> If I can take a plea and walk out now with time in as sentence, why wait around for trial and not know. (Public Defender, Lower Court)
> A defense attorney may back away from a plea saying, "I can't plead my client guilty—the range of possible sentences is too vast." What he really is saying is that he wants some expression from the court as to what the sentence might be—not even what it actually will be. (Judge, Superior Court)

Most court officials agree that pleas usually favor a guilty defendant:

> For a house burglary, if he (the defendant) won't take a plea, he'll probably get indicted. At a trial, if he has a record, he'll get a long sentence. (Public Defender, Lower Court)

It is worth noting the phrase in the above quotation, "take a plea." Although the plea of guilty is frequently thought of as something the defendant offers to the court through his/her attorney, in reality the plea is often structured by the court, according to the court's values and norms, and is accepted or "taken" by the defendant.

Contrary to popular belief, the recommendation of the probation department (in the form of a presentence report) is frequently, if not usually, bypassed in the court's desire to use the certainty of sentence as an inducement for a plea. Although the judge is more inclined to set "ceilings" (i.e., maximum sentences rather than minimum sentences), s/he is "in no way bound by the recommendation of the Probation Department; it's a guideline" (Judge, Superior Court). This judge then noted the case of a man pleading guilty to Manslaughter: "He's prepared to go to prison, but wants to know the maximum sentence he'll serve." The recommendation of the Probation Department, coming after the judge has given a sentence commitment in exchange for the plea, is likely to be used at the judge's discretion in helping him to set a minimum sentence.

Counteracting the Overcharge

Most interviewees acknowledged a tendency on the part of the police to "overcharge" some offenses; sometimes to accumulate "credit" for a felony arrest (which may help in promotion to the rank of detective) and other times mistakenly in a hasty appraisal of evidence (overestimating drug weights or the amount of force used in a purse snatch).

In many instances felony arrests are made by the police because they want a good arrest record so that they can become detectives . . . to get credit to show a supervisor . . .a plainclothesman looking for a gold shield. No one gets into the narcotics squad on aptitude or intelligence, but basically on arrests made of a certain nature and type. (Public Defender, Lower Court)

Whatever the intent, one potential consequence of an overcharge is to allow the prosecutor bargaining flexibility while giving the defendant the appearance of getting a "break."

No doubt a Jury may realize that the evidence does not fit the charge. But the court, acting as a plea-inducing system, often *assumes* that position from the outset and structures this assumption into the plea negotiations:

It's traditionally known that both the DA (prosecutor) and the police overcharge. It's not done maliciously but because it makes a better chance for a disposition—any disposition—since you can always remedy an overcharge. (Private Defense Attorney)

Alschuler's interviews with prosecutors and defense attorneys around the country uncovered the "elaborate sham" of the court-legitimized overcharge:

In a sense, overcharging and subsequent charge-reduction are often the components of an elaborate sham, staged for the benefit of defense attorneys. The process commonly has little or no effect on the defendant's sentence, and prosecutors may simply wish to give defense attorneys a "selling point" in their efforts to induce defendants to plead guilty.[19]

In other words, the overcharge is an accepted "tactic," a strategy for inducing pleas of guilty which is maintained and legitimized by the court.

Consolidating Charges

A court's caseload is more easily disposed of by offering to consolidate multiple charges into one charge or multiple cases into one case. Thus, the court makes it possible for the defendant who has been arrested on several cases to enter one plea of guilty to cover several or all of them. . .

> *Case 304.* Defendant charged with defacing and removing identification marks from a stolen automobile. Case merged with another charge pending on Possession of Stolen Property. Indicted by the Grand Jury for Grand Larceny I, Criminally Buying and Receiving Stolen Property, Criminally Concealing and Withholding Stolen Property, and Defacing and Removing Identification Marks. Pleaded Guilty in the Superior Court to Possession of Stolen Property as a misdemeanor.

. . . or to enter a plea of guilty to one "count" of an indictment to cover the entire indictment.

> *Case 221.* Defendant indicated on Assault I, Assault II, Possession of Dangerous Weapon (gun) in a bar brawl. Pleaded guilty to Assault II in the Superior Court and received a three-year probation as sentence.

> *Case 542.* Defendant indicted on Robbery I, Grand Larceny II, Assault III, Possession of a Dangerous Weapon (as a misdemeanor). The case involved the robbery of a liquor store with a knife. The defendant pleaded guilty to Robbery III (unarmed) and received one year confinement (until 18th birthday).

> *Case 306.* Defendant indicted for Grand Larceny I (involving a stolen auto), Criminally Buying and Receiving Stolen Property, and Criminally Conceal-

ing and Withholding Stolen and Wrongfully Acquired Property. All were felony indictments. The defendant pleaded guilty to Petit Larceny and received probation for one year.

Although many factors are involved in the dispositions and sentences agreed upon in the cases illustrated above (e.g., the defendant in *Case 306* had only one prior conviction record), they do not mitigate the role played by the consolidated charge as an inducement to plead guilty. Consolidation allows the prosecutor bargaining flexibility and the defense the appearance of getting a "break."

The "Management" of Dismissals

Abraham Blumberg refers to the drop-out of felony cases at different stages of prosecution as "the sieve effect":

... initially its (the sieve effect) escape holes are somewhat broad and coarse. They begin to sift in an increasingly finite manner as we move structurally from the initial point of police handling to the court of preliminary hearing, then to the arena of the criminal court where felonies are tried. There the process almost freezes, and only infrequently from then on can the accused free himself from the procedural engine.[26]

Universe statistics for 1967 in Metrocourt reveal that approximately 84 percent of cases of the ten offense categories studied were screened out before arraignment in the Superior Court. Only 7 percent of the felonious assault cases reach arraignment in the Superior Court, 13 percent of the burglaries, 3 percent of the criminal possessions, 35 percent of the drug-abuse cases, 9 percent of the frauds, 70 percent of the homicides, 8 percent of the larcenies, 20 percent of the weapons possessions, 31 percent of the robberies, and 14 percent of the sexual-abuse cases. These statistics indicate a differential screening effect for differing offense categories (that is, different probabilities for a case in an offense category to reach final adjudication in the Superior Court). The combined charges of assault, larceny, and burglary comprise more than 60 percent of arraigned felonies that are adjudicated in the Lower Court (26 percent, 19 percent, and 17 percent respectively), although these offenses represent only 30 percent of those arraigned felonies reaching adjudication in the Superior Court. On the other hand, cases brought to court and arraigned for drug abuse, robbery, and homicide comprise approximately 21 percent of all arraigned felonies in the Lower Court, but comprise 57 percent of those cases arraigned in the Superior Court.

In summary, *the data suggest a screening process which differs according to offense category; some arraigned felony offenses are more likely than others to reach final adjudication in the Superior Court.*

Sample statistics reflect this screening effect; offense categories are differentially represented at different stages of final adjudication (Table 3-2). For example, assault cases comprise 45 percent of the sampled offenses adjudicated in Lower Court I (prior to Grand Jury arraignment), while they comprise only 12 percent of the sampled offenses adjudicated in the Superior Court. On the other hand, drug-abuse cases are found in relatively high percentage among cases closed in the Superior Court (29 percent), and comprise only a small percentage of cases closed in earlier court stages. Sexual-abuse offenses constitute a relatively high percentage of cases dismissed by the Grand Jury, along with weapons possession and homicide cases. These statistics support the contention that different offenses follow different routes to final adjudication.

Why does case screening take place? It is safe to assume that not all defendants are guilty of the charged offense, or that evidence is not available to convict every defendant who is, in fact, guilty. The plea utility of the police overcharge (and the prosecutorial overindictment) has previously been acknowledged. Procedural irregularities may account for case dismissals and pleas as well: illegal search and seizure, inappropriate line-up for witness identification of the defendant, a coerced confession. Victim and complainant lack of cooperation is certainly a factor.

Table 3-2
Stage of Felony Adjudication by Offense Category

Offense Category	Sample Statistics, 1967, Metrocourt (percentages)			
	Lower Court I	Lower Court II (returned by Grand Jury)[a]	Grand Jury – Dismissal	Superior Court
Assault	45.0	38.3	13.7	12.4
Burglary	15.0	12.2	6.9	8.3
Criminal possn.	6.0	–	3.9	4.2
Drug abuse[b]	3.0	4.9	5.9	29.1
Fraud	5.0	1.2	5.9	2.1
Homicide	–	–	12.7	8.3
Larceny	20.0	7.4	11.8	8.3
Weapons possn.	3.0	7.4	10.8	4.7
Robbery	2.0	16.0	12.7	19.2
Sexual abuse	1.0	12.3	15.7	3.1
Total	100.0	100.0	100.0	100.0
	(N=100)	(N=81)	(N=102)	(N=193)

[a]Cases sent to the Grand Jury and returned to the Lower Court for disposition.
[b]Drug statistics are inexact because an unknown percentage of these offenses are brought directly to the Grand Jury without lower court arraignment.

When the Rational Actor Model is applied as an explanatory framework, however, the above question (Why does case screening take place?) becomes: How does the court utilize case screening to realize its objective of administrative efficiency? The court acts in the capacity of manager, "allowing" certain cases to reach adjudication by plea or trial, and other cases to be dismissed. By both intent and default, the court, with the assistance of prosecution, influences case dismissals. Warrants, adjournments, and renewed investigations can all be used in the service of avoiding or assuring a dismissal.

Table 3-3 indicates that the complainant plays an important role in case dismissals. For cases dismissed in Lower Court I (prior to Grand Jury presentation), 74 percent of the complaints were withdrawn by the complainant, and the complainant did not appear in court to testify in another 13 percent of the cases. For those cases dismissed in Lower Court II (returned to the Lower Court after Grand Jury presentation), these reasons are reversed in order; 47 percent of the dismissals result from complainant nonappearance and 16 percent from withdrawn complaints.

Legal officials believe that such factors as defendant restitution, and the "cooling down" of feelings after the criminal incident, largely account for these withdrawn complaints and missing complainants. A maxim of court operation was also uncovered which pertains to the large percentage of nonappearance reasons given in Lower Court II: the longer a case is open, the less advantageous for the prosecution. Increasingly disinterested complainants and witnesses, and the recession of memory help to decay a once strong prosecutorial case (also

Table 3-3
Reasons for Felony Case Dismissals in the Lower and Superior Courts

| | Sample Statistics, 1967, Metrocourt | | |
| | % Stage of Adjudication | | |
Reason for Dismissal	Lower Court I	Lower Court Return II	Superior Court
Prima facie case not made	–	–	25.0
Complaint withdrawn	73.0	16.7	–
Complainant not appear	13.5	46.7	–
On request of prosecuting attorney	8.1	20.0	25.0
Referred to narcotics program	–	–	50.0
Referred to youth bureau	2.7	6.7	–
Sentenced on another offense	2.7	3.3	–
Removed to another court	–	3.3	–
Prosecution not ready	–	6.7	–
Total	(N=37)	(N=31)	(N=4)

partially explaining the "on request of the prosecuting attorney" statistic). The statistic representing prosecutor requests accounts for such things as manpower shortages and the resulting priorities.

Does knowing this defeat the argument that the court decides what happens in most cases? Not at all; the court need not maintain a posture of passivity in a dismissal. The high percentage of cases dismissed may indicate the court's unwillingness to utilize techniques available to it to avoid some dismissals.

Adjournments are often used by the defense to "wear down" complainants and witnesses, according to most prosecutors. Yet they can also be used by the prosecutor to avoid a dismissal, as is clear from daily observation of the prosecutor, who, more than any other legal official, reflects judicial policy:

Observation. February 28, Office of the Prosecutor, Lower Court Division. Problem with lady with stolen ring. Perpetrator won't talk, can't get the ring, so have no real case, says the assistant prosecuting attorney. Head of division says "no dismissal"—adjourn case until get more evidence. Expresses confidence in the detective with the complainant (lady) by saying, "I know you'll do a good job."

On the other hand, the prosecutor who does not "block" continued adjournments may be aiding a defense attorney in search of a dismissal:

Observation. February 19, Arraignment Part, Lower Court. At 9:40 every day the court takes Attorney's Applications—before the new arraignment and calendar is called there's a line of defense attorneys before the court clerk, judge, and prosecutor. They all have cases scheduled to come up on the calendar today. They want an adjournment; witness may be unavailable, may not like the presiding judge, may need more time to prepare, may be representing a case in another court. . . . If there have been two or three previous adjournments on the case the prosecutor might ask it be noted on the record that this will be the last adjournment. When the case comes up again it will be dismissed if people are still missing.

When there is notice of a "last adjournment" date in court, the bench can issue a "bench subpoena" (that is, a subpoena which informs the relevant individuals in the case when and where to appear to give testimony). Behind this subpoena lies the threat of "contempt of court" if the summoned individual does not appear. In addition, a subpoena can be delivered with "personal service" (that is, the subpoena is delivered personally so that the receiving individual cannot say he has not received it).

Since the offense of assault comprises the largest percentage of dismissals in the Lower Court (only two percent of all sample cases were dismissed in the Superior Court), all cases of assault which were dismissed because of the failure of a complainant to appear in court or because of the withdrawal of a complaint were reviewed. In no case was the subpoena used in an attempt to induce a complainant to continue the case.

Reasons given for dismissals by the Grand Jury were largely evidentiary. Approximately 45 percent were for "insufficient evidence"; 17 percent were classed as "justifiable, excusable"; 9 percent were listed as "no evidence of conscious knowledge of illegality"; 7 percent were for "culpability of both parties"; 6 percent were for "credibility of the complainant at fault." While dismissal reasons are no doubt valid, it should be noted that the Jury is controlled to some extent by the presentation of the case by the prosecuting attorney . . .

The prosecutor can do whatever he likes with the Grand Jury. (Prosecuting Attorney, Superior Court)
     In the Grand Jury only the prosecutor presents evidence. That is the problem. A lopsided situation. (Judge, Superior Court)
     The trick before the Grand Jury is to impress upon them the law and suggest, without telling them, what to do. (Otherwise) you might get an indictment you didn't want. (Prosecuting Attorney, Grand Jury)

. . . and direction given by the office of the prosecuting attorney:

An assistant (prosecutor) who knows what the hell he's doing can make them (the Grand Jurors) do whatever he wants. But if I thought the case was a piece of garbage and I wanted to get rid of it, I'd have to consult (his division head). (Prosecuting Attorney, Superior Court)
     A prosecutor is not worth his salt unless he can play the Grand Jury as a violin. (Prosecuting Attorney, Grand Jury)

The prosecuting attorney quoted above then proceeded to recall an "accident" which occurred in the Grand Jury the previous day:

He (the assistant prosecutor) should have seen that the Jury didn't indict. Just yesterday he went in to the Jury and "flubbed the dub." He didn't follow orders. (Prosecuting Attorney, Grand Jury)

Although some Grand Jury dismissals may result from an "accident" of a prosecutor not "following orders," the point is that Grand Jury dismissals (as well as returns to the Lower Court and indictments headed for the Superior Court) represent "management" by the court and prosecutor to an unknown degree.
     A case which is dismissed by the Grand Jury—or the Lower Court—may be rectified through resubmission to the Investigations Bureau of the prosecuting attorney upon prosecutorial or judicial advice . . .

Observation. February 28, Office of the Chief Assistant Prosecuting Attorney.
Looked over an abortion case pending. It was dismissed in the Lower Court on a technicality (police didn't show up at the right time and day). He's (the

prosecutor) in the midst of reviewing the court papers and deciding whether to act on them. He can either accept the dismissal or send the papers to (the division head) in the Investigations Bureau, or (the division head) in the Grand Jury.

. . . or resubmission to the Grand Jury for presentation:

> *Case 306.* Defendant arrested for Criminal Possession of Stolen Property (auto). Case dismissed in the Lower Court due to complainant not appearing. When contacted by the prosecutor it was discovered that the complainant had been to court several times before without results. Promised he will appear before the Grand Jury if summoned. . . . Case presented to the Grand Jury and defendant indicted on Grand Larceny I. Case is adjudicated by a plea of guilty in the Superior Court—to Petit Larceny.

To summarize, just as the plea of guilty is utilized by the court for purposes of administrative efficiency, and inducements are structured for the offer of a plea of guilty, court dismissals can be partially understood as the result of intentional, purposeful decisions made by the court. The use or lack of use of adjournments, subpoenas, and case-investigation techniques can be viewed as management devices for case screening.

Although administrative efficiency needs dominate court action, system constraints exist and operate to create "rational boundaries." One such constraint may be the legal code, another, available resources, and a third, community expectations. In other words, to understand the full complexity of case adjudication, concepts and models are needed in addition to those introduced in the Rational Actor Model. The following chapter discusses the Organizational Process Model and focuses on informal procedures and norms of case "worth," which are adhered to by court personnel, offering another perspective in explaining court behavior.

Notes

1. Graham T. Allison, *Essence of Decision.* Boston: Little, Brown and Company, 1971. In the context of decision-making during the Cuban missile crisis, Allison discusses the Rational Actor Model, organizational model, and bureaucratic models of decision-making.

2. Ibid., p. 20. Reprinted by permission.

3. Ibid. This summarizes Allison's position.

4. Wayne LaFave, *Arrest: The Decision to Take a Suspect into Custody.* Boston: Little, Brown and Company, 1965.

5. Donald J. Newman, *Conviction: The Determination of Guilt or Innocence without Trial.* Boston: Little, Brown and Company, 1966.

6. Omitted are cases (1) receiving special youthful-offender treatment, (2) where no finding is made, (3) where a case is transferred to another jurisdiction, and (4) where a charge is consolidated with another case.

7. *The Challenge of Crime in a Free Society,* The President's Commission on Law Enforcement and Administration of Justice. Washington, D.C.: U.S. Government Printing Office, 1967.

8. "The Importance of the Defendant's Plea in Judicial Determination of Sentence," *Yale Law Journal,* 66, 1956, 204-22. Concern with administrative efficiency is also voiced in "Official Inducements to Plead Guilty: Suggested Morals for a Market Place," *University of Chicago Law Review,* 32, 1964, 167-87.

9. Ruth Weintraub and Rosalind Tough, "Lesser Pleas Considered," 32 *Journal of Criminal Law and Criminology,* 1942, 506-30.

10. Samuel Dash, "Cracks in the Foundation of Criminal Justice," *Northwestern University Law Review,* 46, 1951, 385-406. For the author's later acceptance of the plea process as the "nerve center" of justice, see Samuel Dash, "The Emerging Role and Function of the Defense Lawyer," *North Carolina Law Review,* 47, 1969, 598-632.

11. *The Challenge of Crime,* op. cit.

12. Donald Newman, op. cit.

13. A *corum nobis* proceeding is for an alleged error in fact, not appearing on the record, in order that the court may correct the error which it is presumed would not have been committed had the fact been brought to the court's notice in the first instance.

14. American Bar Association Project on Standards for Criminal Justice, *Standards Relating to Pleas of Guilty.* Chicago: American Bar Association, 1968, p. 9. Used by permission.

15. This sentiment is echoed by Albert Alschuler (p. 71) in his study of the prosecutor's role in plea bargaining: "[plea bargaining] is a more flexible method of administering justice. It affords a far greater range of alternatives than do most trial proceedings." Albert Alschuler, "The Prosecutor's Role in Plea Bargaining," *University of Chicago Law Review,* 36, 1968-69, 50-111.

16. Felonious assault was the only charge category with enough cases to make the within-offense comparison worthwhile. Lower Court trial convictions equaled nine in the sample. Lower Court pleas of guilt equaled twenty-one.

17. *Standards Relating to Pleas of Guilty,* op. cit. Used by permission.

18. "The Importance of the Defendant's Plea in Judicial Determination of Sentence," op. cit.

19. Albert Alschuler, op. cit.

20. Abraham Blumberg, *Criminal Justice.* Chicago: Quadrangle Books, 1967, p. 51. Copyright 1967 by Abraham S. Blumberg, First New Viewpoints Edition published 1974 by Franklin Watts, Inc. Used by permission.

4   Adjudication by Agreement

The Rational Actor Model's explanatory power derives primarily from viewing action chosen by an organization as the best alternative, when consequences are viewed in relation to objectives. The court, from this perspective, is a monolithic entity, and its actions are assumed to be based upon known alternatives and consequences.

At a different level of analysis, the group interactive level, an organization can be viewed as a coalition of subgroups with disparate demands which result in a series of de facto agreements that impose constraints upon the organization. The existence of such agreements in court has been commented upon by Sudnow, in his account of the manner in which the public defender prepares and conducts a defense: the public defender and prosecuting attorney have institutionalized a common orientation to allowable reductions.[1] Demythologizing the adversary nature of the court, adjudication can be viewed as institutionalized evasions of due process under law which arise from informal agreements reached between all concerned parties (defense, prosecution, bench). According to Blumberg, accused individuals come and go in court, but the structure and its personnel remain to carry on their respective career, occupational, and organizational enterprises.[2]

The "common orientation" and "informal agreements" reached among legal officials can be used to explain felony adjudication by focusing on disposition and sentencing statistics. Legal officials, to a large extent, react in similar fashion to similar defendants and cases. A case in which a defendant beats up his/her spouse, for example, is viewed similarly by different subgroups within the court.

This chapter outlines the basic assumptions and principles which underlie the Organizational Process Model. Discussion focuses on dispositions and sentences given in specific instances and the informal normative system shared by legal officials.

The Organizational Process Model

The daily operation of the court evolves from the actions of three important subgroups: prosecution, defense, bench. Reaching most decisions involves representatives from each of these groups. Disposition and sentencing statistics highlight the interweaving of subgroup behavior and reflect those internal organizational processes which result in decision-making. The internal dynamics of each subgroup are largely overlooked by the Rational Actor Model, which reduces such complexities to the behavior of a single actor with a single motive for choice of action.

Realizing the extraordinarily difficult requirements placed upon understanding an organization's actions by the Rational Actor Model (e.g., generating all possible alternatives, assessing all possible consequences), Herbert Simon developed a theory of "bounded rationality" which deviated from the Rational Actor Model in many ways.[3] Viewing the complexity of organizational problems, Simon noted that every organization must subdivide its problems into numerous parts, which are then dealt with by quasi-independent organizational subdivisions. Since all organizations do not have the capacity to uncover all possible alternatives and consequences, they must make do with a course of action which suffices. This means that an organization can stop at the first alternative which satisfies ("satisficing"). The "search" behavior which finds this alternative is generated by a stable, routine process instigated by the organizational subgroups. Much of this behavior is based upon avoiding uncertainty in the future.

Simon's concept of bounded rationality (that is, choices which are constrained by realistic organizational problem-solving needs) was extended by Cyert and March,[4] who focused on organizational decisions in terms of organizational goals and expectations. Their theory assumes that there is no internal consensus within an organization at the level of operational goals. Conflicts do occur, which are resolved by acting on problems as they occur. This entails developing standard operating procedures for the actions of each subunit so that an uncertain future does not result.

The Organizational Process Model synthesizes the concerns of these organizational scholars and introduces the notion that interacting subgroups with partially divergent interests "meet" these divergent demands.

The basic assumptions and concepts of the Organizational Process Model can take the form of propositions:

1. The operational goals of an organization are seldom revealed by formal mandates. Rather, each organization's operational goals emerge as a *set of constraints* defining acceptable performance.
2. Internal consensus between organizational subgroups does not necessarily exist at the level of operational goals.
3. As a problem arises, the subgroups of the organization most concerned with the problem deal with it in terms of the constraints they take to be most important.
4. Given divergent constraints, subgroups within an organization avoid uncertainty by arranging a *negotiated environment*. By doing so they regularize the reactions of actors with whom they have to deal.[5]

The preeminent feature of this model is that organizational activity is determined by the establishment of standard operating procedures and norms agreeable to organizational subgroups as defining acceptable performance.

Reconsider the question posed for the Rational Actor Model: Why are cases screened out of court? The Organizational Process Model analyst need not seek the best overall rationale to explain this occurrence; rather, the analyst assumes that subgroups of the court operate independently, and proceeds to examine interests, demands, and needs that are specific to each subgroup. To what needs is the prosecutor responsive? Asked in another way, what would be the political repercussions of mass dismissals due to poor case work-up because of "no time" for the serious cases? What are the concerns of the defense? While the concerns may be individual clients, what is the balance struck between attorney fee expectations and reputation and the need to turn over cases quickly? What are the expectations placed upon judges—by the public, which oversees elections and budgets, by court administrators, who oversee case assignments and case flow, and by higher courts, which oversee decisions through the appeal mechanism?

Each subgroup reacts with its own set of internal constraints, which are based upon differing goals and priorities. However, in order for decisions to be made and actions taken, the Organizational Process Model states that these differing needs must be accommodated, mediated, negotiated, or traded off so that each subgroup has a chance to realize some desirable goal.

When applied to the court setting, activity involving subgroups is based upon informal agreements concerning processes and norms which simplify decision-making and limit adjudicatory uncertainty. Although each legal subgroup works within its own varying set of interests and constraints, their functional interdependence in the process of adjudication, and their basic agreement upon the necessity for efficiency in court administration, promote the emergence of consensus on case evaluation; that is, shared norms of adjudication. In other words, the institutionalized common orientation that Sudnow observed between the public defender and prosecuting attorney is the operationalized equivalent of the organizational concept of a "negotiated environment."

Socialization for Consensus

How does a prosecutor, defense attorney, or judge learn the "appropriate" objectives and attitudes of his/her subgroup? Each subgroup has its own methods of inculcation, some more direct than others, some continuing for a longer time period than others. The offices of the prosecutor and legal-aid attorney offer, perhaps, the most formalized and continuous settings for attempts at socialization of subgroup concerns, procedures, and norms.

The Office of the Prosecuting Attorney

Individuals joining the Office of the Prosecuting Attorney as assistant prosecutors bring with them a wide range of skills and experiences, not all of which prove relevant in their new position. In many prosecutors' offices, the assistant is recently graduated from law school, and using this first position to gain experience. Although Metrocourt had its share of novice attorneys, most of these prosecutors interviewed had some work experience before joining the staff:

BH was a private defense attorney having some contact with Metrocourt over a four-year period after graduation from a local law school. He had been with the prosecutor's staff for six years.

AW graduated from a local law school and worked for a firm specializing in maritime law for five years. He engaged in one year of private practice (civil and criminal) before joining the prosecutor's staff. He had been there eleven years.

SG, after graduating from a local law school, worked in the negligence field for six months before coming into the prosecutor's office ("never having been in criminal court before or having a case of my own"). He had been with the office for seven years.

PC worked for the legal department of an insurance firm for several years after law-school graduation, and had a private criminal practice for three years before joining the staff of the prosecuting attorney.

The newcomer to the office is given an overview of office functions by the chief assistant prosecutor and division heads and typically begins an "apprentice" position in the Investigations Bureau before working himself "up" to higher court sections, ultimately to the trial section of the Superior Court. For example, new prosecutors in the Investigations Bureau will "ride homicide" with more experienced attorneys, sit in when statements are taken from witnesses and complainants, and have assigned to them an experienced attorney who is available for calls and questions on a twenty-four-hour basis. When considered ready to have his own cases, this novice's "advisor" may question him about his activities and decisions, or observe him functioning both in and out of the office.

A similar process of socialization takes place in each division of the prosecutor's office, insuring relative uniformity in procedure and judgment. After a period of observation, the new attorney in the Lower or Superior Court is given easy cases (cases which are straightforward, routine), and observed handling them. In both courts, the new and inexperienced attorney is advised to consult the division chief in questionable cases, and must consult that superior before a case is dismissed:

No one in the office will turn down a plea if it's sensible and we can justify it with our superiors. (Prosecuting Attorney, Superior Court)

Some (prosecutors) won't reduce, indict, or do anything before talking to . . . (division chief). Most go to them for dismissals. I want another opinion where I might be criticized. It's protective. I'll usually make a decision first and go tell . . . (division head) to see if he agrees or disagrees. It's office procedure to report a dismissal. If it's approved, you're covered. (Prosecuting Attorney, Lower Court)

Internal mechanisms within each organizational division monitor an assistant prosecutor's courtroom activities:

Every day of the week I get a disposition sheet on what happened in court—all parts . . . we aren't as concerned about an individual's record, except for dismissals and acquittals. (Prosecuting Attorney, Superior Court)

Informal policies established by the head of the office for the entire staff, or by a division chief for his own department, are learned by direct teaching, discussions over coffee, and at weekly staff meetings:

Every murder case we have in this office, there is a conference on. We have conferences on cases we feel are important. They may hit the newspapers, headlines. They may deal with public policy. (Prosecuting Attorney, Superior Court)
    In the Lower Court there's a one-for-two rule: if there are several arrests you take a plea for one and dismiss the others. (Prosecuting Attorney, Lower Court)
    At the start of every month—sometimes week—the heads of the division sit down with all the cases and talk about each one to see which indictment can be reduced, which stays. . . . (Prosecuting Attorney, Grand Jury)

Direct instructions from division chiefs to assistants in each court section can be observed in the form of notes written on the flaps of case folders, which are passed from prosecutor to prosecutor as a case moves through different stages of adjudication:

Case 277. No plea less than Attempted Burglary III unless approved by . . . (division head).

Case 278. . . . (Prosecutor in Lower Court) offered Attempted Burglary III—refused. Stay with this offer. (Signed by previous prosecutor)

Case 355. Defendant must plead guilty to indictment or go to trial. (Signed by division head)

Since a prosecutor will remain in one division for months or years, he soon becomes "specialized" in that division. A prosecutor who reaches the Superior Court trial section has had experience handling cases in almost every other court section:

BH's Office Profile: Complaint Division, two weeks; Investigation Bureau, six months; Grand Jury, two years; Superior Court Trial, four years.

IC's Office Profile: Complaint Bureau, three months; Investigations Bureau, one year; Lower Court, four months; Grand Jury, one year; Superior Court, two months.

Movement through the office divisions depends both on whether a prosecutor is considered "ready" for the next "higher" division and whether there is an opening available.

The Defense Attorney

Office of the Public Defender. The Office of the Public Defender is structurally similar to that of the Office of the Prosecuting Attorney. The manner of socializing the public defender into office policy and procedure is similar. The head of the Lower Court division of the office pointed this out:

. . . (Head of Lower Court for Prosecutors) has the same problems I have with new attorneys. We try to give them lectures, give them reading materials, after-work conferences. . . . (Public Defender, Lower Court)

The formalized introductory period is complemented with informal office dynamics:

We swap information, we confer, we're a close-knit group. We have absolute discretion as an attorney, [sic.] but we try to pass on information to help each other. (Public Defender, Lower Court)

The public defender who is a novice is as aware of his/her initial inexperience as is the division chief:

In the beginning you don't know. You believe everything they (the defendants) say. Take it at face value. But after one or two bloopers you get to know. (Public Defender, Superior Court)
There's no hard guidelines, but you get reactions and the office feeds you suggestions. The only hardcore rule is "no plea of not guilty." (Public Defender, Lower Court)

It is interesting to note that a large proportion of the public defenders in Metrocourt find their way to the office, as the prosecutor does, after a few years of working in other phases of law:

JK graduated from a local law school and spent two years in a private insurance practice. He had been with the public defender office for six years.

AC spent six months working for the Federal Bureau of Narcotics and then spent eight years rotating through all divisions of the legal-aid office. He is now attached to the Superior Court division.

LD practiced law for twelve years as a private attorney (generalist) and joined the public-defender staff four years ago.

PR was in negligence work for three years, corporate work for one year, and had been working with the public defender for one and one-half years.

To summarize, the public defender is socialized into office routines and norms in a manner similar to that of the prosecuting attorney. These attorneys specialize by court section, and look forward to upward mobility within the office hierarchy by either working their way into the Superior Court division or attaining a division-chief position.

The Private Attorney. The socialization of the private defense attorney into the court "system" (i.e., procedures and norms) comes either through trial and error in case representation or through having been previously socialized into one of the court's subgroups. The following are profiles of private defense attorneys who frequently represent cases in Metrocourt:

LW has been a solo practitioner (mostly criminal work) for the past forty years.

MC, after graduating from a local law school, spent six years on the police force, and six months as a detective for the office of the prosecuting attorney before establishing a private (criminal) law practice.

LC is a former prosecuting attorney, in solo defense practice for the last four years.

JS followed a year of solo private practice (generalist) with three years as a public defender. He is presently in private practice.

The frequently appearing, experienced private attorney is considered at an advantage in case representation:

When you get a good, well-known lawyer, the tendency on the part of the prosecutor is to give a better plea. . . . (Private Attorney)
The former prosecutor knows what he can get and that helps him. . . . Former prosecutors are usually good attorneys for their clients because they know the police and the prosecutor's weaknesses. (Prosecutor, Lower Court)

The infrequently appearing attorney—the one less known by the court—is handicapped by his lack of familiarity with informal court procedures and norms:

He may have less experience and not be aware of the areas in which he can more successfully negotiate. He may conclude his defendant is guilty. When the prosecutor offers him a plea he may feel it's a good thing for his client, while another lawyer will sit down and tell him (the prosecutor) he can't really convict on his information—and they'll begin to negotiate. (Private Attorney)

In sum, the socialization of the private attorney takes place through a previous affiliation with a court subgroup (e.g., former prosecuting attorney) or through a private practice which takes him into court frequently as a solo practitioner. The private defense attorney learns through "trial" and error, rather than through a formalized socialization process (although we observed such attorneys coming to the office of legal aid for advice on case matters). In a limited partnership (a two- or three-man office), socialization into court procedures and norms is readily available; here the attorney is able to share information about the court and seek advice and opinions within the confines of his own "shop."

The Judge

A judge is either elected to the Lower Court for a six-year term or appointed to the Superior Court for a term of fourteen years, with the understanding that s/he will be endorsed for a second term by both political parties. Background profiles of some of the judges interviewed reveal great variation in their familiarity with the criminal court before appointment to the bench:

Judge D graduated from law school in 1937 and practiced civil law for two years. He became secretary to a judge in the state court of appeals for four years and then secretary to a chief judge in a federal district court for six years. He was elected to the Lower Court on a two-year opening and appointed to the Superior Court.

Judge C was secretary to a mayor of the city, then secretary to the Board of Education. He was a solo private practitioner (general practice) for thirteen years prior to being appointed to the Lower Court.

Judge R was state legislator for seventeen years, where he was chairman of the penal-code committee and the gun-control committee. He was in private practice as a civil attorney during these years and received a judicial appointment five years previous to this interview.

Judge H was in private practice (general) for fifteen years before becoming a prosecuting attorney. As a prosecutor he rotated through almost every division including the position of assistant to the chief prosecutor. After a four-year term as chairman of a state athletic commission he became a Lower Court judge (four years). He is presently a Superior Court judge.

Perhaps because many judges come to the bench without courtroom experience, attorneys and prosecutors are often critical of their knowledge of the law, their concern for "justice," or their ability to evaluate a case.

Although no formal "training" takes place, it appears that judges become specialists in a court section due to the formalities and informalities of judicial rotation. One prosecuting attorney commented that "a judge who can't, or won't, plea bargain, will never be put in ... (the conference and discussion section)." Although judges are generally rotated through several court sections (within the Lower Court or within the Superior Court), remaining one month in each, a judge who "does well" in a particular part may find himself sitting there for most of the year.

Judicial performance is monitored predominately by a chief administrative judge who ask questions: Are cases kept moving? How many decisions are appealed? How many defendants sentenced to probation return to court on another charge? Although not in daily contact with an "office" and the directives of a division chief, a judge's relationships with members of the other subgroups both in and out of court (e.g., in political, fraternal, or religious groups) result in informal socialization into his expected role.

Reaching Consensus

The Organizational Process Model accepts differences between court subgroups, in terms of goals, needs, constraints. It stresses, however, the need for agreed-upon operating procedures and norms to carry out daily activities. According to the data, such agreements seem to be advantageous to each subgroup. The prosecutor, for example, while seeking to take the highest disposition possible, also suffers the uncertainties of pressing for trial, by questioning his own abilities to convict . . .

If I felt from the Grand Jury and a trial he (the defendant) would get one to three years, or two to four years (for a burglary of a store) I'd go back to the reasoning that "a bird in the hand. . . ." In between here (the Lower Court) and the trial (in the Superior Court) we have twenty-three people in the Grand Jury and twelve more in the trial. We have to convince thirty-five people that this guy is guilty. (Prosecuting Attorney, Lower Court)

. . . his witnesses . . .

How is your witness going to stand up? He's nervous. He may say something not true. I had a case where I knew his testimony—I didn't pay him or coach him—but he made a mess of trying to tell the whole truth. When I get a guy on the stand I can't put words in his mouth. (Prosecuting Attorney, Lower Court)

. . . his evidence . . .

What about a defendant who tells us how he killed a person but the police officer can't testify, for it's illegal evidence. Should we let him walk the streets? We compromise. (Prosecuting Attorney, Superior Court)

In other words, the plea process, for the prosecutor, reduces the uncertainty of trial outcome and assures a guilty disposition. Coupled with informal departmental policies on pleas, the entire process is legitimized:

Assault and robbery, assault with a deadly weapon, house burglary, sale of drugs—we try not to take a plea on these cases. (Prosecutor, Lower Court)

The defense attorney also seeks to limit case uncertainties. His concerns may result from a strong case against his client . . .

They'd accept a plea readily because most narcotics cases are open and shut (sale to an undercover police narcotics agent). (Prosecutor, Superior Court)
If my guy is a dead loser, why should I go to trial? I'll take the best plea I can get. (Private Defense Attorney)

. . . limited trial experience . . .

A good criminal practitioner may get only five trials per year in the Superior Court. (Private Defense Attorney)

. . . personal handicapping qualities of his client . . .

Some defendants, no matter what they say, it won't come out well. And the case may ride on the individual once he takes the stand. (Private Defense Attorney)

. . . his client's prior conviction record . . .

Cases are patterned right away, according to certain variables. . . . A previous record always hurts the defendant, especially in trial. (Private Defense Attorney)

. . . or an "in" he has with the court which makes the trial mechanism all the more hazardous a procedure . . .

I can talk their (prosecutor and judge) language. I can sit down openly with a prosecutor and know where I can go with a case—the outer limits. (Private Defense Attorney)
Public defenders are a power unto themselves and they get away with murder. They've been given a position that has proven Frankensteinian for the court. (Judge, Lower Court)

The judge in Metrocourt is "judged" largely by how he "moves" his cases. According to one Superior Court prosecutor, voicing a statement frequently heard from others, "they (the judges) are playing a numbers game—move your case, move your calendar." Since a judge is "judged" largely on the basis of a statistical report (number of cases adjudicated and number of cases appealed), according to another Superior Court prosecutor, "the only way to show they've done a lot of work is by the number of cases tried and the number disposed of per week." This prosecutor then offered an example of how, for statistical purposes again, some judges will "give the courthouse away" and attempt to involve the prosecutor—to cover themselves:

Let's say a promise of a sentence is given for an armed stick-up of a drug store. The defendant has a record. I want Robbery III but the judge already made a deal for three years. The judge now wants as low a plea as he can get to justify his promise of a sentence (the prosecutor must accept the plea). In case the defendant commits another crime and the newspapers go after him he can say "I only gave him . . . because he pleaded guilty to . . . and the prosecutor accepted the plea. He knew more about it than I did. . . ." I have to do right by the public. If it's a stick-up and should be Robbery II, the sentence is the judge's responsibility. If he wants to kiss him (the defendant) goodnight and put him to bed, he does what he wants. (Prosecuting Attorney, Superior Court)

Each judge receives a weekly statistical report which indicates whether he's "getting the job done," according to a prosecuting attorney:

If they don't get a good record they feel badly about it. We'll get a call (chief of the division) saying that the assistant (prosecutor) in the part isn't cooperating. Most of the time it's not the prosecutor's fault—he knows values, what the pleas should be. (Prosecuting Attorney, Superior Court)

A private defense attorney indicated that "the pressure on the judge of his own workload may be a deciding factor in a case."

In summary, the socialization process which members of each subgroup undergo, combined with their mutual needs to avoid the trial mechanism, result in a situation which favors a negotiated environment in terms of the Organizational Process Model. This negotiated environment, characterized by a method of deciding cases and the norms upon which decisions are based, is evident in interactions both within and without the courtroom.

Subgroup Interaction Outside the Courtroom

The constant informal interaction which takes place between and among the subgroup members outside the courtroom is easily observed. The following record, covering a two-hour period in the office of the chief assistant prosecuting attorney, clearly reveals the broad range of interaction of this prosecutor, as well as the informality with which cases are discussed and decisions are made:

Observation. February 28, Office of the Chief Assistant Prosecuting Attorney. Fiscal officer comes in to ask about new desks for offices. Jokes about the prosecutor being an interior decorator.

Judge on telephone asking about a specific case—an embezzler who fled to another state. He has to decide whether or not to extradite.

Private defense attorney comes in to ask the prosecutor his opinion on a homicide case he is representing in the Superior Court.

Prosecutor talks with fiscal officer about civil-service positions and hiring a particular man whose qualifications are unclear.

Chief of Superior Court prosecutorial division stops in for an opinion on how to proportion assistant prosecutors in his division on different cases.

Private defense attorney (who, according to the prosecutor, "goes to trial a lot") stops by to say "hello."

Prosecutor signs checks and payroll.

Assistant from the Investigations Bureau comes in to discuss a case dismissed in the Lower Court. It had been returned to the Investigations Bureau for further work.

Prosecutor speaks on phone with a private defense attorney assigned to a case by the court. Gives him his opinion on case handling.

Prosecutor speaks on phone with legal-aid attorney in the Lower Court who wants to acquaint the prosecutor's office with his defendant. The attorney says his defendant is "a good kid" and wants to "save him." Prosecutor says he'll OK giving him YCB (Youth Council Bureau) for a long-term parole.

Prosecutor speaks with someone in reference to a withdrawn complaint, involving an extortion case in which the complainant withdrew his complaint for a fee. Prosecutor says that "the office won't encourage this," but will accept it.

The following record also covers a two-hour period in the office of the head prosecutor of the Lower Court division:

Observation. February 29, Office of the Division Head, Lower Court. Prosecutor comes in to see the division head about a case that will be dealt with "adversely to the state's interests" since there will probably be a dismissal. He wants to talk about it soon.

Police officer comes in and asks for advice on taking court action when an arrest hasn't been made.

A "mistake" walks in looking for the Complaint Division.

Private defense attorney wants to talk about an unexpected racial issue that has come up in his case.

Division head speaks with someone on telephone about dismissing a charge, but is afraid something will happen if they do.

Friend of division head walks in and introduces a "friend who has a problem." The friend needs YO (Youthful Offender) treatment for someone.

Police come in and ask what to do in a situation where a witness doesn't want to testify in a case.

Division head telephones to a prosecutor to call a specific case right away and dismiss it.

A few irate prosecutors come in. One won't speak because I'm sitting there. The other wants to lock up someone. It is approved.

A woman, originally a complainant, comes in about a countersuit in which she is now a defendant. She doesn't think she should have been arrested because it's a disgrace to her name, her reputation is being dragged through the gutter, and now she'll have a record. She is advised to get a lawyer and have him bring out the facts in court.

Detective comes in with a witness in a case. He wants a "release" for a statement of testimony so that the witness doesn't have to appear in court again. The "release" is written.

The above observations reveal the informal way in which "business" is often done; prosecution, defense, and bench are in daily interaction, reaching accord outside the courtroom. Cases are discussed over the telephone, case-management advice is passed along between individuals representing theoretically opposing groups. In terms of the Organizational Process Model, these informal discussions between subgroup members both establish the ground rules for decision-making and legitimize them. The functional interdependence of these groups is highlighted more clearly, however, through the following discussion of courtroom interaction.

In-Court Exchanges between Subgroups

A major concern of the Organizational Process model—the need to create routine, standard operating procedures, a negotiated environment—is implicit in Blau's theory (or "prolegemenon of a theory," as Blau refers to it) of social-exchange behavior.[6] Blau defines social exchange as the voluntary actions of individuals that are motivated by the returns they are expected to bring and typically do in fact bring from others. Exchange behavior, Blau continues, is based upon the existence of mutual dependence, shared expectations, and anticipated rewards.

Each of these conditions is implicit in the Organizational Process Model, and underlies the need for agreement between court subgroups on case management and outcome.

One element which distinguishes Blau's discussion of social exchange from real courtroom behavior is the *form* of sociation upon which the discussions are based: Blau refers to two-partner liaisons (whether individual-to-individual, individual-to-group, group-to-group) while most courtroom interaction involves the participation of three groups. This triadic relationship, when it occurs, brings with it an important difference from that of the dyadic: superordinate and subordinate relations are altered. The addition of a third "partner" may devalue the impact of the individuality and power of any one partner or enhance the power of any one partner through coalitions.

There is no doubt that individual idiosyncrasies and abilities play a role in case management and outcome:

The personality of the prosecutor plays a large part in dealing with the defense attorney. Some are always fighting with him. (Judge, Superior Court)

Some judges are really bigoted. Like saying, "You know those kinds of people. . . ." (Private Defense Attorney)

There are differences in their (prosecutors') ability to evaluate. Some have a feel and sense of a case without reading it. Some are bright, some are dull. Some are pigheaded no matter what the judge says. (Judge, Superior Court)

Law is not understood by some judges. The law may have nothing to do with the court. It's who is trying the case. (Private Defense Attorney)

It is for some of the above reasons that judge-shopping or the use of adjournments as case-management techniques occur. One public defender boasted that defenders get better and more pleas because "we can arrange cases, maneuver them so we can shop around." On the other hand, the same holds true for the private attorney, according to one prosecutor: "They'll wait out the complaint and judge-shop. Since they're in court daily they'll delay a plea as long as possible. . . ."

Attempts are made, however, to counteract these idiosyncracies. A higher plea may be insisted upon to control the range of sentences when in the hands of an "easy" judge:

Certain judges will give the court away for nothing. I wouldn't offer the same plea in front of those judges I know will sentence easy. You're compromising as a prosecutor, in a plea—so you must consider the sentence. (Prosecuting Attorney, Lower Court)

In the same manner, a judge may refuse to accept a plea that seems too low (in the Superior Court a plea to a lesser charge must be accepted by the judge as well as the prosecutor):

Generally, the prosecutor and I go along. But I may not take a plea if I feel it's too low. So I'm also the boss to that degree. (Judge, Superior Court)

Recourse to a higher authority is always possible:

If I ever had a quarrel—felt a prosecutor was arbitrary, capricious, I could go to his superior. Not for a slap on the wrist, but for the defendant, and appropriate action is taken if my case holds up. (Public Defender, Lower Court)

It was previously noted that prosecutorial policy may act to counteract idiosyncratic behavior and decisions: recall the messages written on the outside of case folders which define the precise plea acceptable or specify the appropriate range of acceptable pleas.

Although individual differences exist, are known to courtroom regulars, and are manipulated in an attempt by each subgroup to achieve its own objectives, understandings exist which cut across these groups and exert great pressure toward routine and regularity. These understandings will be discussed in a later section. Documented in this section are the predominant forms of subgroup interchange which emerged from observational and interview data: competition, mediation, and arbitration. Each form can and does take place at any stage off adjudication, although "arbitration" is more likely found in the conference and discussion section of the Superior Court.

The critical distinction between these forms is the role the judge chooses to play in case adjudication. Judges "operate" in differing ways. Some judges will not discuss a plea of guilty at all, leaving all arrangements up to the prosecutor and defense attorney. All this type of judge will do is accept the plea when recommended by the prosecutor. Other judges will participate in discussions to a limited extent; but the discussion is strictly confined to the facts and merits of the case, with case resolution left to the prosecutor and defense. This type of judge will not discuss a possible sentence, an element viewed as critical by many defense attorneys. The third type of judge involves himself completely in discussion, and uses his sentencing ability to influence case outcome.

Competition. Competition exists when the judge, as third partner, does not take an active role in helping the prosecution and defense agree upon an appropriate disposition and sentence. This form, then, does not differ markedly from any dyadic relationship. It is found primarily in the Lower Court, or outside the conference and discussion part of the Superior Court. To illustrate: The defense attorney initiates a discussion of a case and its potential, suggesting a disposition (and/or sentence) acceptable to his/her client. The prosecuting attorney rejoins with his perception of case factors and either agrees with defense evaluation or demands or suggests a counteroffer. Agreement is either reached after continued negotiation or the case is marked to continue to the next stage of adjudication. The judge's role is conspicuously absent.

This form of behavior may take place outside of the courtroom . . .

Observation. February 28, Office of the Division Chief, Lower Court. Defense attorney comes in to ask for a reduction he thinks the prosecutor at court might not want to give him "on the spot." He wants to "clear it" ahead of time. He discusses the case with the division chief, and the chief places a call to the prosecutor in the court part.

. . . or within the court . . .

Observation. February 28, Arraignment, Lower Court. Prosecutor announces jokingly that this is "bargain day." Discusses with a defense attorney what to do with a weapons-possession case. They talk a bit and decide that one of the defendants will take the charge for the weapon and drugs found and the case against the other defendant will be dismissed. The first defendant pleads guilty.

Sex-abuse case in which a little girl was molested twice by the same teenager as she was waiting for the school bus. Father of the teenager, a psychiatrist, comes up to speak with the prosecutor and tells him that rather than send his son to the hospital until his case comes up, "where he really won't get any treatment because he'll be declared legally sane," he would like to have the boy put on parole so he could receive psychiatric care. Prosecutor speaks to the defense attorney, then to the judge. It's agreed.

In the above example, the judge plays little or no role in case decision-making, despite the fact it involves accepting a plea or continuing the case.

Mediation. Another behavioral form exists in which the judge guides the process of decision-making. In the role of mediator, arguments made by each attorney are objectified, realistic alternative resolutions are presented, but never is a position taken or an attempt made to impose resolution on prosecutor or defense. Similar to the role played by Simmel's nonpartisan mediator, the judge ". . . produces the concord of two colliding parties, whereby he withdraws after making the effort of creating the direct contact between the unconnected or quarreling elements."[7] Observations highlight this form of interaction:

Observation. March 3, Hearing, Lower Court. Judge in this court appears aggressive. He's closely questioning the defense attorney, and detectives. Seems to be leading the prosecutor to speed things up. Announces to court that they should be quiet. . . . Judge asks to see the papers the prosecutor is reading. Asks the narcotics official what he wants to do about the case—is quite directive. Consults a legal code about the case to check on law (first time I've seen a judge refer to a book of any sort). Judge calls the prosecutor and defense attorney up to the bench to decide and discuss. Prosecutor and defense reach agreement and present it to judge. Judge seems to accept, and calls father of complainant up to bench to talk about the problem and what they feel is the best disposition to help the defendant and the new situation.

New case is called. Prosecutor and defense both in hallway interviewing witnesses, preparing them for questions to be asked in the courtroom. Prosecutor talking with police about the case. Private attorney has been retained for one defendant and public defender for another. Confession. Police inform public-defender attorney that his client "is a dummy"; he helped someone move stolen property for all of $10. No malice on part of police. . . . In court, private attorney wants to adjourn—complainant not present. Public defender wants to go ahead—his client has been in jail one month thus far. Judge adjourns case and sends it back to calendar part for new date. . . . Public defender and prosecutor confer. Return to hearing room after next case is heard. Convince judge to hear case. After prosecutor and defense present their respective cases, judge takes over questioning, looks at ballistics report, etc. Public defender wants a dismissal of the charge—says prosecution did not establish case on all counts. Prosecutor says he'll dismiss the weapons charge, but not the stolen-truck charge. Judge asks if this is agreeable to both of them. Agreement reached.

It should be emphasized that mediation seems to be based upon the judge's ability to remain detached from the partisan interests and opinions of the attorneys. Problems are likely to arise when the judge allows objective elements to influence his judgment, when nonpartisanship is doubted by one or the other partner:

The private lawyer's friendship with a judge will affect the judge and might affect the prosecutor's outlook on the case. (Public Defender, Superior Court)

Public defense will do better than I . . . they have a working relationship with the judge and know the people in court. But private attorneys who hook up with judges will do better. (Private Defense Attorney)

A "hook up" between a judge and a defense attorney which is disguised as bipartisanship can occur in all three forms of adjudication, but is more important in mediation and arbitration, where the judge plays a more active role in case determination.

Arbitration. A major difference between competition, mediation, and arbitration is that in the latter form the judge plays an active, and often determining, role in case resolution. This usually entails the judge's willingness to offer a sentence promise at the time the defense offers a guilty plea (i.e., prior to receiving the probation department's presentence report):

... in the final analysis you are interested in the sentence. You might even say to the judge that you're interested in seeing this man on probation and you'll take whatever label he wants. (Private Defense Attorney)

This (knowing the sentence) is the most important feature of the conference and discussion. When I was a defense attorney and wanted to plead my client guilty, I would never do it with my eyes closed. Attorneys want some indication of what the sentence is likely to be. (Judge, Superior Court)

Invariably the client asks you, "What happens if I plead guilty to . . . ?" (Private Attorney)

When the judge will stipulate as to the sentence, on the record, it's easier to accept a plea. (Private Defense Attorney)

It is interesting to note that the attorneys who expounded upon the need for the known sentence were most often the private defense attorneys. The reasons for this will be discussed in the following chapter.

Arbitration is most likely to take place in a court part specifically set aside for negotiation:

Observation. March 25, Conference and Discussion Part, Superior Court Case 1. Defendant indicted on Assault I and Possession of a Dangerous Weapon. Prosecutor reads papers in his folder in presence of defense attorney and judge. Before defense speaks the prosecutor "offers" him Assault III. Attorney ignores the offer, tells his defendant's story. He believes his client did find the gun in a wastebasket and it fired accidentally. Judge says the case is only worth a misdemeanor—for weapons possession. Judge offers a sentence of probation and asks the prosecutor and defense if this is agreeable. Agreement is reached and defense attorney leaves to bring his client into the room.

Case 2. Private defense attorney presents his case to the judge, informing him what he thinks his client deserves. Judge nods his head in agreement. It appears that both the judge and the prosecutor know this defense attorney well. Group discussion. They quickly decide on Assault III (a misdemeanor) and a sentence of probation. Defendant is brought in.

Case 3. Defense explains his case, indicted on Assault II. Says he "wants to bargain." Prosecutor looks at his sheets and says there seems to be more in the case than the attorney admits. Attorney agrees. Prosecutor continues that fact have been omitted and that the defendant may be unreliable. Defense responds. Prosecutor seems annoyed at flippancy of the attorney, turns to him, saying, "You know who the judge is," and that "you should have come in with the bargain already prepared." Attorney says he'll go out and speak with his client.

The above dialogue does not take place in a vacuum. Most negotiations in the conference and discussion part appear to rest upon understood rules and roles. Unwillingness to behave according to expectations (as in the last observational notation) may affect present and future personal relationships as well as eventual case outcome.

The "play" in an interaction is more important than who speaks first and who responds. Although by law the prosecutor controls the acceptance of a plea: "I can't give a plea if the prosecutor doesn't consent" (Judge, Superior Court), the judge controls the setting of the sentence: "These days we make sentence promises; I'm the only one who can do that" (Judge, Superior Court), and the defense controls offering the plea: "It's not our job to twist anyone's arm to take a plea" (Public Defender, Lower Court). Case decision-making is a relatively free-form interaction in all of the above forms (i.e., competition, mediation, arbitration). And the entire process seems to be able to continue *despite* the existence of a defendant:

If there's an absence of the defendant we can talk freely. I take the attitude that we're the experts. We know the law, the prosecutor has evidence and the attorney (defense) talks to the defendant. We (three) should sit as a committee and try to figure out the best thing. (Judge, Superior Court)

No one remembers defendants, only lawyers. You know the judge, cops, stenos—no one knows the defendant. He's always in the way. He don't know the business. The jerk that don't know the business gets in everyone's way. It would be better if they weren't around. (Prosecuting Attorney, Superior Court)

Case Adjudication

On the basis of the socialization which takes place, both within and between subgroups, and the constraints of each subgroup's activities which serve to promote "understandings" regarding dispositions and sentences, it readily follows that such agreements exist and are recognized by subgroup members as a necessary and important part of adjudication. Cases are neither disposed of in a random manner nor with sole regard for the penal code and available evidence. Rather, *case disposition is based largely upon institutionalized agreements on allowable reductions.* Both dispositions and sentences given for specific offenses reflect these agreements. From the perspective of the Organizational Process Model, disposition and sentencing statistics are outcomes of the negotiated environment.

Dispositions. Few cases charged and arraigned as felonies in the Lower Court are adjudicated as felonies. Only 16 percent of all cases arraigned as felonies in Metrocourt reach final adjudication in the Superior Court, the only court in which a felony disposition can be levied.

Given this high screen-out rate between the Lower and Superior Courts, what happens to cases *within* each court? Table 4-1 documents the percent of each offense category which is adjudicated as dismissed, misdemeanor, or felony in both the Lower and Superior Courts, revealing differences between offense categories in their likelihood of adjudication in the Lower Court or Superior Court and their dispositions in each court. For example, the offenses of assault, burglary, and sexual abuse are likely to be adjudicated in the Lower Court; the offenses of drug abuse, homicide, larceny, and robbery are more likely to be adjudicated in the Superior Court. Regarding specific offense dispositions, approximately 60 percent of Lower Court assaults are dismissed or acquitted; approximately 87 percent of Superior Court robberies are adjudicated as felonies.

This table indicates that only half the cases adjudicated in the Lower Court are adjudicated guilty of a misdemeanor (51.9 percent); the other half are dismissed or acquitted (48.1 percent).[8] Once a case is indicted by the Grand Jury and arraigned in Superior Court, few dismissals or acquittals occur (6.1 percent). More than half the cases (56.7 percent) adjudicated in the Superior Court are adjudicated guilty of a felony, while the remaining cases (37.2 percent) are adjudicated as misdemeanors (an adjudication which could have been made in the Lower Court as well).

Approximately 60 percent of the assaults adjudicated in the Lower Court are dismissed or acquitted; the respective percentages for the offenses of robbery and sexual abuse are 60 percent and 45 percent. Superior Court statistics reveal that burglaries are likely to be given a felony disposition (81 percent), and the assault and drug-abuse cases are equally as likely to be disposed of as a misdemeanor or as a felony. A relatively high proportion of homocide and sexual-abuse cases (18.7 percent and 16.7 percent, respectively) have their charges dismissed. In short, discrepancies between original offense charge and final offense disposition exist which are offense-specific.

When this information is viewed in conjunction with the information in Table 4-1, a picture of felony adjudication in Metrocourt emerges which indicates that *different offenses have different probabilities of reaching a specific stage of adjudication (i.e., Lower Court, Grand Jury, Superior Court) and of receiving a specific disposition (i.e., dismissal, misdemeanor conviction, felony conviction).* To illustrate: few drug-abuse offenses are adjudicated in the Lower Court (3 percent of all felony arraignments, Table 3-1), but those that are adjudicated in this court are likely to be found guilty of, or plead guilty to, a misdemeanor (71 percent of all drug adjudications). The relatively large proportion of drug offenses which reach the Superior Court for adjudication are

Table 4-1

Case Disposition by Stage of Adjudication

| | Sample, Metrocourt, 1967 (percentages) | | | |
| | Disposition | | | |
Stage of Adjudication	Dismissal/ Acquittal	Misdemeanor Conviction	Felony Conviction	Totals
Totals				
Lower Court[a]	48.1	51.9	–	(N = 156)
Superior Court	6.1	37.2	56.7	(N = 194)
Assault				
Lower Court[a]	60.5	39.5	–	(N = 76)
Superior Court	7.7	50.0	42.3	(N = 26)
Burglary				
Lower Court[a]	37.5	62.5	–	(N = 24)
Superior Court	6.3	12.5	81.3	(N = 16)
Criminal Possession				
Lower Court[a]	33.3	66.7	–	(N = 6)
Superior Court	–	62.5	37.5	(N = 8)
Drug Abuse				
Lower Court[a]	28.6	71.4	–	(N = 7)
Superior Court	3.6	52.7	43.7	(N = 55)
Fraud				
Lower Court[a]	–	100.0	–	(N = 6)
Superior Court	–	50.0	50.0	(N = 4)
Homicide				
Lower Court[a]	–	–	–	(N = 0)
Superior Court	18.7	–	81.3	(N = 16)
Larceny				
Lower Court[a]	–	100.0	–	(N = 2)
Superior Court	–	50.0	50.0	(N = 16)
Weapon Possession				
Lower Court[a]	22.2	77.8	–	(N = 9)
Superior Court	–	100.0	–	(N = 9)
Robbery				
Lower Court[a]	60.0	40.0	–	(N = 15)
Superior Court	10.5	2.6	86.9	(N = 38)
Sexual Abuse				
Lower Court[a]	45.4	54.6	–	(N = 11)
Superior Court	16.7	50.0	33.3	(N = 6)

[a]Includes cases initially adjudicated in the Lower Court and those cases sent to the Grand Jury and returned to the Lower Court for disposition.

given dispositions split almost equally between misdemeanors (52.7 percent) and felonies (43.7 percent). A similar analysis could be undertaken for each offense category and would reveal trends highly individual to that offense category.

Assessing Case Seriousness. The differential adjudicatory and dispositional patterns in each court, for specific offense categories, result from a variety of factors, some of which are legalistic (i.e., factors based in formal procedural and substantive law) and others of which are extralegal (i.e., factors which exist alongside the formal codes). Both sets of factors play an important role in the daily operation of the criminal court. For example, in Newman's study of the various components of nontrial adjudication and the practices employed by judges and prosecutors he finds that legal evidence for full prosecution of a defendant may be available, but for a number of sociopolitical reasons the prosecutor may decide to reduce the charge or the bench may decide to dismiss it.[9]

The extralegal factors, however, are of particular interest to the Organizational Process Model, a model which views consensus among subgroup members facilitating decision-making by routinizing activities, and limiting uncertainty in case outcome by establishing outcome expectancies. The "common orientation" and "informal agreements" commented upon earlier are used by legal officials for this purpose. Understandings regarding *case seriousness* comprise one set of informal agreements. The following sections will comment upon how case seriousness is determined by Metrocourt's subgroups.

The concept of case seriousness, as viewed by the legal officials of Metrocourt, has two prominent aspects: (1) the potential violence inherent, or actually present, in an offense; and (2) the perceived threat of the offense to the community of reference. For heuristic purposes, seriousness can be visualized as the intersection of two coordinates (Figure 4-1). The *violence potential* ordinate ranges from minimum to maximum and is defined as actual or potential physical harm to an individual. Potential or actual violence may range from tolerable to intolerable along the "threat to community" ordinate. To determine case seriousness the court relies upon the perceptions and attitudinal values of legal

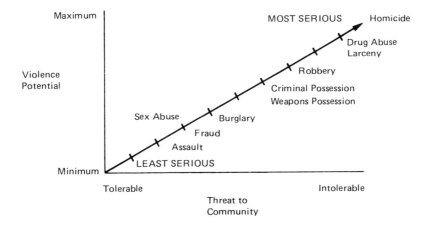

Figure 4-1. Between-Offense Comparison of Offense Seriousness

officials: (1) to decide which *community* is the referent group (e.g., Hispanic–American community), and (2) to assess the degree of *tolerance* for particular behaviors that take place within that community by community members.

In the terminology of the Organizational Process Model, a negotiated environment evolves among legal officials in the form of a common orientation to case assessment. Case seriouess becomes a relevant constraint in decision-making. For instance, when legal officials were asked about those factors that influence adjudication, a typical first response focused on whether or not there was a potential for violence:

Robberies are generally not reduced to misdemeanors. House burglaries, where there's a potential victim confrontation, aren't either. But car thefts, where kids are on a lark and there's no violence, are reduced all the time. (Private Defense Attorney)

If a man has been convicted of a vicious crime (meaning violence was involved) . . . he needs to be put away. (Public Defender, Lower Court)

Reductions depend upon potential for personal injury for a victim—and on planning. (Private Defense Attorney)

Most judges have antipathy to crimes of violence. (Private Defense Attorney)

Crimes of violence are treated more severely in law and in plea bargaining. (Public Defender, Superior Court)

Wolfgang and Ferracuti have pointed out that the use of violence has differing meanings for differing subcultures.[10] In some subcultures the use of violence is expected in certain situations and is part of the shared normative system. The same behavior, transferred to a different subcultural setting, may be socially unacceptable.

In addition to the importance of potential violence, Metrocourt officials refer to the meaning an act has for a particular referent community:

They (the defendants and victims) live by different values. You have to go by the way they live. We must recognize their standards. (Judge, Superior Court)

The judge then illustrated his point with a case of homicide resulting from a drinking situation:

They'll spend money for liquor and then fight over who drank more. Take a homicide resulting from a simple stabbing of a friend—but the wound wasn't taken care of. . . . He's dead; his survivors know it's one of those things. He'll (the defendant) take a Manslaughter plea and an assault sentence. (Judge, Superior Court)

The critical words in the above quotation are "they" when used in relation to a "simple stabbing" that is just "one of those things." The following statements echo the point more clearly:

People who get arrested are not up to middle-class standards. They're different. (Private Defense Attorney)

A poor ghetto girl is sexually violated and has an illegitimate child. You can't expect her to adhere to our morals. (Judge, Lower Court)

The point being made is that court officials perceive certain criminal behavior (as defined in the criminal code) to be relatively acceptable forms of interacting in "certain" communities. *These legal officials share a common orientation to case assessment which focuses on the concept of "seriousness" and not upon the specifications of the criminal code.*

Between-Offense Comparisons. The disposition statistics presented earlier can be ranked along a "seriousness" continuum, according to likelihood of adjudication in the Superior Court (Figure 4-1). Interpreted as a reflection of offense seriousness, the offenses of homicide, drug abuse, larceny, and robbery are likely to be perceived and evaluated as serious by legal officials and adjudicated primarily in the Superior Court. Similarly, the offenses of assault and sexual abuse are likely to be perceived and evaluated as less serious and adjudicated primarily in the Lower Court. Although the majority of assault cases involve violence, their form and nature are perceived by legal officials as tolerable to the referent community, and the assault case is adjudicated primarily in the Lower Court. In contrast, homicide is never viewed by legal officials as a tolerable offense, and all cases in the sample are sent directly to the Grand Jury and are typically adjudicated in the Superior Court.

When sample statistics are ordered according to likelihood of final adjudication in the Superior Court, the following ranking occurs:

homicide

drug abuse

larceny

robbery

criminal possession

weapons possession

burglary

sex abuse

fraud

assault.

The offenses of homicide, drug abuse, larceny, and robbery are adjudicated primarily in the Superior Court (over 50 percent of each offense category). In contrast, the offenses of assault, fraud, and sex abuse are most likely to be adjudicated in the Lower Court. Does this mean that all assault and sex-abuse cases are considered less serious than drug-abuse and robbery cases? Not necessarily. The role legal evidence plays in case disposition can sometimes be critically important: the sex offense, which by law needs corroborating evidence independent of the complainant, never reaches or succeeds with the Grand Jury. Particular prosecutor-office policy may determine dispositions: drug-abuse cases, irrespective of case particulars, are by prosecutorial policy sent to the Grand Jury. In other words, while offenses can be rank ordered according to likelihood of final disposition in the Superior Court, each offense category, in its own right, needs to be understood in order to apply the concept of case seriousness to that offense.

Within-Offense Comparisons. While it is instructive to compare perceived case seriousness between offense categories (e.g., robbery, assault), the schema is helpful in exploring within-offense discriminations in case seriousness. For example, the large proportion of assault cases not reaching the Superior Court suggests that these cases either did not involve violence, or that the violence involved (actual or potential) was perceived by legal officials as tolerable to the referent community. The large percentage of assault dismissals (60 percent) suggests that many defendants were falsely charged or that evidence was not available to reach an adjudication of guilty. Neither conclusion is correct. When the offense of assault is controlled for victim-offender relationship an interesting pattern emerges: assaults on a police officer are less likely to be dismissed (14 percent) than are assaults on a stranger (50 percent), and the latter are less likely to be dismissed than are assaults on a friend or relative (73 percent). These data are presented on Figure 4-2. These more detailed statistics suggest that an assault in which the victim and perpetrator are members of the same community is viewed as being less serious than a similar case in which the participants belong to different communities. But continued exploration indicates that even this conclusion is inaccurate. The following statements reveal why:

It's a (ghetto) type of crime. Puerto Ricans are at a christening party and a fight over a wife. Someone picks up something and the district attorney prosecutes the winner. You never get the true story. (Judge, Lower Court)

A stockbroker who shoots his wife for adultery will get a stiff sentence. A black man who shoots his girl friend for adultery may get three years. (Private Defense Attorney)

In other words, Puerto Ricans are viewed by the court as a community within which an assault is part of the life-style. As long as such behavior remains within the community, according to legal officials, it is perceived as tolerable by legal agents and considered nonserious. The stockbroker, on the other hand, is perceived as part of a community which does not tolerate violent behavior. In

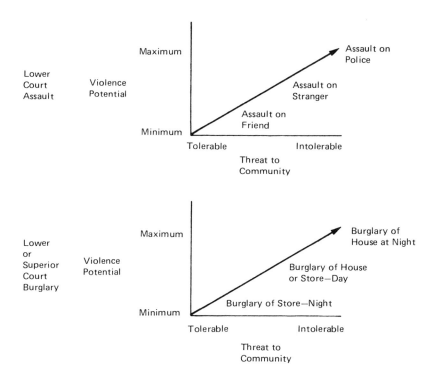

Figure 4-2. Within-Offense Comparison of Offense Seriousness for Assault and Burglary

other words, violence *is* perceived by the courts as acceptable in some communities.

Assessing seriousness of the burglary offense is largely related to the time and location of the offense.

Three kids break into a garage. There's a good chance a plea will be taken to a misdemeanor because the premises were empty and would have remained empty all night. The odds were small that someone would get hurt. But with a burglary in a house where people were asleep I'd set bail at $2,500 each because the defendant is a menace and could have attacked the residents. (Judge, Lower Court)

Assessing case seriousness through informal agreements quickens the "negotiated environment," in terms of our model, quickens the pace of adjudication, and limits case-outcome uncertainties by narrowing the range of available dispositional alternatives. Sudnow's concept of "normal" crimes (cases in which typical features are attributed to offenders and offenses)[11] is readily extended into a concept of "normal case dispositions" (defined as routine case dispositions based upon informal agreement among legal officials regarding case seriousness).

Sentences. Sentences for cases adjudicated guilty in Metrocourt are presented in Table 4-2. Sentences have been ranked in leniency according to categories of nonconfinement, confinement of one year or less, and confinement of one year or more. The assumption exists that either unconditional or conditional probation is the most desirable sentence of the three listed. Interviews in Metrocourt indicated that being "on the street" is always preferable to being confined.

For the defendants convicted of, or pleading guilty to, an offense in the Lower Court, 68.1 percent are sentenced to confinement of less than one year. It should be remembered that a misdemeanor disposition cannot carry with it a term of confinement in excess of one year. The remaining 31.9 percent of the defendants' cases are not confined (receiving unconditional discharge, probation, or time served). For the Superior Court sample, 47.5 percent of the defendants convicted of, or pleading guilty to, an offense are sentenced for one year or longer, 13.8 percent are sentenced for one year or less, and 38.7 percent are not confined.

Ironically, a larger percentage of cases adjudicated as misdemeanors in the Superior Court are likely to receive nonconfinement sentences (37.2 percent (N=72)) than are cases adjudicated as misdemeanors in the Lower Court (31.9 percent (N=39)). Although this difference is small, the fact that both courts are similar in their nonconfinement sentences implies that better sentencing "bargains" are struck in the Superior Court than in the Lower Court, given the "stiffer" sentencing possibilities in the Superior Court. Although better bargains may often result from weak evidence against a defendant, the situation is just as

Table 4-2
Case Sentences by Stage of Adjudication

| | Sample, Metrocourt, 1967 (percentages) | |
| | Stage of Adjudication | |
Sentence	Lower Court[a]	Superior Court
Nonconfinement	31.9	38.7
One year confinement or less	68.1	13.8
One year confinement or more	–	47.5
Totals[b]	(N=81)	(N=181)

[a]Includes cases adjudicated in Lower Court and those sent to the Grand Jury and returned to the Lower Court.
[b]Excludes dismissals and acquittals.

likely to arise from the "threat" of a felony trial; the need to negotiate seriously becomes more important as the possibility of a trial draws nearer, leading to dispositions and sentences in the Superior Court which were improbable in the Lower Court.[1,2]

Superior Court statistics are especially interesting because the "stakes" or "ante" is higher. Although nonconfinement (probation) and sentences of less than one year are available, this court is the only one in which the possibility exists of confinement for longer than a year, according to real differences in the length of sentences authorized for different offenses. Disposition/sentencing discrepancies in the Superior Court, for selected offenses, are presented in Table 4-3. For example, 86.7 percent of the burglary offenses adjudicated in the Superior Court were found guilty of a felony; 81.3 percent of the sentences given to convicted burglars were for confinement of more than one year (the sentence by which a felony offense is defined). Thus, there is a hiatus of only 5 percent between felony adjudication and felony sentencing. This statistic can be compared with assault, which reveals a gap of 29 percent between felony adjudication and sentencing. Comparisons can be made with the other offenses as well.

The following discussion points to what may be a pattern similar to that found in disposition statistics; specific offenses differ in their "favorableness" of sentencing.

On what bases can sentencing differences between offenses be understood? When asked to list variables prominent in the sentencing decision, legal officials' responses ranged from the sentencing structure of the penal code . . .

Before the change in the penal law, the sentencing structure for felonies was more rigid. Many times a person (defendant), because of rigidity, even if he wanted to go to trial, couldn't afford to take the chance. (Judge, Superior Court)

. . . to the sentencing philosophy of an individual judge . . .

I am a great believer in probation, wherever possible. No one is rehabilitated in the prison setting. Out of 100 on probation, I may get back one or two. And if he violates probation, I have simply to send him to jail—quick, cheap. (Judge, Superior Court)

. . . to the demands placed on the court by related criminal-justice agencies . . .

When jails get overcrowded and the Commissioner of Corrections calls up . . . it's pressure on everyone. (Public Defender, Lower Court)

The importance of a defendant's prior conviction record in the sentencing decision was noted, however, by almost every legal official:

Table 4-3
Dispositions and Sentences by Offense Category in the Superior Court

Offense Category	Dispositions[a]	Sentences	Totals
Sample Statistics, Metrocourt, 1967 (percentages)			
Assault			(N = 24)
Misdemeanor	41.2		
Felony	58.8		
Nonconfinement		54.2	
One year confinement or less		20.8	
One year confinement or more		25.0	
Burglary			(N = 15)
Misdemeanor	13.3		
Felony	86.7		
Nonconfinement		6.3	
One year confinement or less		12.5	
One year confinement or more		81.3	
Homicide			(N = 13)
Misdemeanor	—		
Felony	100.0		
Nonconfinement		15.4	
One year confinement or less		—	
One year confinement or more		84.6	
Drug abuse			(N = 53)
Misdemeanor	54.7		
Felony	45.3		
Nonconfinement		35.8	
One year confinement or less		18.9	
One year confinement or more		45.3	
Larceny			(N = 16)
Misdemeanor	50.0		
Felony	50.0		
Nonconfinement		62.5	
One year confinement or less		12.5	
One year confinement or more		25.0	
Robery			(N = 34)
Misdemeanor	2.9		
Felony	97.1		
Nonconfinement		23.5	
One year confinement or less		—	
One year confinement or more		76.5	

[a]Excludes dismissals and acquittals.

A previous record shows he (the defendant) must be caged for the good of the community. (Judge, Superior Court)

A prior record weighs heavily in plea or trial. (Public Defender, Superior Court)

There comes a point where I lose interest in a defendant with a record. You can't salvage him. It's too late. Now you have to watch out for society. (Judge, Superior Court)

Implicit in these quotations is neither an orientation toward retribution nor an attempt to deter others from crime through the use of a sentence of confinement. Rather, they suggest that multiple offenses are seen as a commitment of an individual to a criminal life-style, and the sentence is viewed as one way an individual is prevented from repeated criminal acts. Thus, sentencing in Metrocourt is only grossly related to notions of deterrence or rehabilitation. The "hardened" (repeater) criminal "needs" to be sentenced for the protection of society, although rehabilitation is not expected to take place within the prison setting.

No one is rehabilitated in the setting of prison. But with some cases there's no alternative. These are cases of "hardened" criminals. (Judge, Superior Court)

Since most judges and other court officials agree that there is no ongoing rehabilitation in prison, they prefer to utilize probation for almost all other offenders, but especially for the first offender.

If a guy has never been in jail, I'd fight to keep him out. (Private Defense Attorney)

When sentencing statistics were cross-tabulated with prior-conviction records of defendants, the resulting relationship was statistically significant: that is, defendants with a better record of prior convictions (none or one prior conviction) receive more favorable sentences in both the Lower and Superior Courts.

Although variables mentioned above are no doubt considerations in sentencing, courtroom observations and statements made during the course of interviews with legal officials led to closer examination of the role of the defense attorney. It was confided frequently that an attorney's knowledge of the court process is significant in sentencing and that the defendant is more concerned with his sentence than with his disposition. According to one judge, "It is a crime to allow a civil lawyer to handle a criminal case." Attorneys who are well known to the court and trusted by its legal personnel may be in a more favorable negotiating position:

You'll never change human nature. If I know a lawyer who has been trustworthy, aboveboard, gives me the good and bad of his case, I'll say to him, "This is what the prosecutor has. . . . This is a reasonable plea . . . let's talk about sentence." (Judge, Superior Court)

Similarly, the defense attorney who knows the individual idiosyncrasies of his colleagues may easily and confidently "judge-shop" or "prosecute-shop" for a sentence.

Perhaps the most convincing argument for the importance of the defense attorney in sentencing is the disappearance of the significant relationship between prior record and sentence when the third variable of attorney representation is held constant. (Appendix, Table A-2) The chapter which follows, then, discusses the all-important role of the defense attorney in both case management and outcome.

Notes

1. David Sudnow, "Normal Crimes: Sociological Features of the Penal Code in a Public Defender Office," *Social Problems,* Vol. 12, 1965, 255-76.

2. Abraham Blumberg, *Criminal Justice.* Chicago: Quadrangle Books, 1967. Copyright 1967 by Abraham S. Blumberg, First New Viewpoints Edition, published 1974 by Franklin Watts, Inc. Used by permission.

3. Herbert Simon, *Administrative Behavior.* New York: Free Press, 1976.

4. R. Cyert and J. March, *A Behavioral Theory of the Firm.* Englewood Cliffs, New Jersey: Prentice-Hall, 1963.

5. Graham T. Allison, *Essence of Decision: Explaining the Cuban Missile Crisis.* Boston: Little, Brown and Company, 1971. Reprinted by permission.

6. Peter M. Balu, *Exchange and Power in Social Life.* New York: John Wiley and Sons, 1967.

7. Kurt H. Wolff, ed., *The Sociology of George Simmel.* New York: Free Press, 1950, p. 22.

8. Acquittals account for 15 percent of this statistic.

9. Donald J. Newman, *Conviction: The Determination of Guilt or Innocence without Trial.* Boston: Little, Brown and Company, 1966.

10. Marvin E. Wolfgang and Franco Ferracuti, *The Subculture of Violence: Towards an Integrated Theory in Criminology.* London: Tavistock Publications, 1967.

11. Sudnow, op. cit.

12. In an interesting article which tells the defense attorney "how to" settle a criminal case, Robert Polstein advises the defense attorney that he can force a lesser plea by insisting on a trial. (Robert Polstein, "How to Settle a Criminal Case," *Practical Lawyer,* 8, January 1962, 35-44.)

5   Advantaged Representation

Organizations are not monolithic, either in ideology or in operational procedure. Differences among organizational actors in roles, responsibilities, perceptions, and priorities permit each to focus on different aspects of a complex issue. What determines a course of action is not simply agreed-upon goals and facilitating organizational routines and understandings. The power and skill of proponents and opponents contribute to shaping the course of action.

Research on differential class justice has highlighted differences between different types of defense attorneys in their ability to represent a client favorably, often concluding that the indigent defendant who relies on representation by the public defender receives legal assistance which is inferior to that received by the defendant who retains an attorney privately. The public defender's youthful age, lack of experience in criminal law, poor compensation, and lack of resources for thorough case preparation and presentation have been offered by legal scholars and researchers as reasons which place the defender's clients at a disadvantage in court.[1] Some studies which focused directly on case dispositions, comparing the public defender with the privately retained attorney, concluded that defendants represented by the public defender more often receive adverse dispositions than those defendants represented by private counsel.[2] Other studies, however, have concluded that one type of defense attorney does not perform better than another, but that each performs a different role in the overall task of adjudication. These studies have reported similar dispositions for the clients of the public defender and the private attorney.[3] Although Oaks and Lehman found that frequency of entering a plea, selecting trial by judge or jury, and obtaining acquittal through trial varied by defense-attorney groups, they speculated that these differences could be explained by differences in clientele, offenses handled, and organizational factors.[4]

The previous chapter highlighted the consensus which exists among legal officials on the adjudicatory "worth" of specific offenses. However, the public defender and private defense attorney work under different organizational and occupational pressures, and are judged successful by different standards and reference groups. For example, the public defender works within a large organization while the private attorney works either solo or in a small partnership. The public defender receives an annual salary while the private attorney receives a fee from each client. These and other differences can be expected to influence role performance and case outcome.

This chapter focuses on defense-attorney case management and case outcome, with the objective of clarifying whether, and which, differences explain the actions of the privately retained attorney and the public defender. Special attention is given to the role played by these attorneys in sentencing, without pretending to consider all of the many legal and extralegal factors which may also play a role in the sentencing decisions. Although the Rational Actor and Organizational Process Models were helpful in interpreting data presented earlier, a model which explains adjudication on the intragroup level of power politics— the Bureaucratic Politics Model—will be referred to in this chapter as the guiding perspective. In this chapter it is assumed that within both the formal constraints and the institutionalized normative system of the court and its officials, some flexibility in decision-making exists. Further, it is differences between defense-attorney subgroups which explain the differences in case outcome.

The Bureaucratic Politics Model

Although the Rational Actor and Organization Process Models were helpful in providing a context for understanding court objectives and the existence of consensus among subgroups which underlie procedures and norms of adjudication, neither model addresses itself to the intragroup and interpersonal level of power politics. The Organizational Process Model's view of court behavior as organizational output, partially coordinated by relatively unified subgroup concerns, provides a differing understanding of the court than found in the Rational Actor's view of court behavior as a choice of a unitary decision-maker. The third model, however, views an individual in each subgroup as an actor in his own right in the court. Decisions are made by individuals who have differing needs and constraints and objectives.

The present chapter focuses on the differences in occupationally related constraints of the privately retained and public-defender attorneys, and offers a third "cut" at understanding courtroom behavior. Anticipated differences which may exist in case outcome as a result of occupational differences highlight the appropriateness of the Bureaucratic Politics Model, which provides a framework for analysis on the level of power politics. The word "court" can be substituted in the following quotations where the word "government" appears.[5]

The decisions and actions of government are . . . political resultants: *resultants* in the sense that what happens is not chosen as a solution to a problem but rather results from compromise, conflict, and confusion of officials with diverse interests and unequal influence; *political* in the sense that the activity from which decisions and actions emerge is best characterized as bargaining along regularized channels among individual members of the government.

. . . rules establish the positions, the paths by which men gain access to positions, the power of each position . . . rules constrict the range of . . . decisions and actions that are acceptable . . . rules sanction moves of some kinds—

bargaining, coalitions, persuasion, deceit, bluff, and threat—while making other moves illegal, immoral, ungentlemanly, or inappropriate.

. . . decisions are made, and . . . actions taken, neither as the simple choice of a unified group, nor as a formal summary of leaders' preferences. Rather, the context of shared power but separate judgments about important choices means that politics is the mechanism of choice. *Each player pulls and hauls with the power at his discretion for outcomes that will advance his conception of . . . interests.* (emphasis added)

The power variable plays an important role in this model, consisting of one's bargaining advantages, skill, and will in using to advantage whatever is needed.

The Bureaucratic Politics Model views each individual in an organization as an individual player. Politics is the game which is played via regular channels among players in different positions within the organization. Decisions, then, are not understood as the reasons that support a course of action, or by organizational routines and standard operating procedures, but by the power and skill of different individuals.

This model of analysis has been used in the fields of political science and interactional analysis, while its appearance in criminological studies is virtually nonexistent. For example, Warner Schilling's study of the politics of national defense[6] looks at budgeting as a political process for which there are no "right" answers, while there are varied differences in opinion on budgeting and a differential distribution of power and advantages among individuals who will be called upon for decisions. Policy, then, results from conflict, coalition, and bargaining. Roger Hilsman's account of foreign policymaking in the Kennedy administration[7] viewed policy as a result of battles among rivals who hold differing power positions in relation to the president, and who had to compete for his ear and support of their opinions through persuasion, accommodation, and bargaining.

Whenever applied, the basic assumptions and concepts of the Bureaucratic Politics Model can take the form of propositions:

1. Decisions are made by a number of individuals (rather than a unitary agent or conglomerate of organizations).
2. Each individual is shaped by his/her own goals, interests, perceptions, and stakes.
3. Each individual stands within a specified power position for any given question or decision. Sources of power might include control of information, the ability to affect other's objectives, personal persuasiveness, and skills.
4. Decisions and actions which are taken are political resultants and reflect the advantages associated with power.[8]

Applied to the criminal court, it is posited that different defense-attorney groups, private and public defender, are "shaped" differently.[9] Do differing defense groups have differing constraints and needs? Do they result in differing court advantages (i.e., power) in client representation? The following discussion highlights those variables which emerged from the data as relevant for understanding defense-attorney behavior in court.

Using Power

Public and private defense attorneys each play a major role in case representation in both the Lower and Superior Courts; each group represents approximately 50 percent of the Lower Court sample, while the public defender represents approximately 40 percent of the Superior Court sample.

Statistics reveal that each attorney group manages its cases differently: (1) cases represented by public defenders are closed more quickly in both the Lower and Superior courts; (2) defendants represented by private attorneys are more likely to be in the community, rather than in jail, while their case is pending further action (Table 5-1); (3) public defenders offer more pleas and private attorneys request more trials in the Lower Court, while the method of disposition utilized in the Superior Court is similar for both attorney groups (Table 5-2). These statistics are particularly meaningful when viewed in relation to the differing contexts within which each attorney type works. The structural constraints of each group's legal practice are highly influential in methods of case management. Differences in caseload, work flexibility, and compensation

Table 5-1
Attorney Group by Bail Status of Client and Stage of Adjudication

	Sample Statistics, Metrocourt, 1967 (percentages)			
	Lower Court		Superior Court	
Status	Public Defender	Private Attorney	Public Defender	Private Attorney
Bail	25.7	41.3	13.1	34.5
Jail	60.0	26.7	78.9	42.2
Released on Recognizance[a]	12.8	32.0	2.6	8.6
No Bail	1.4	–	5.3	14.6
Totals	N = 70	N = 75	N = 76	N = 116
	Chi square is significant at .01 level. Raw chi square is 18.94 with 3 df.		Chi square is significant at .01 level. Raw chi square is 25.23 with 3 df.	

[a]The defendant is released pending hearing on the strength of his/her own good character and the stability of his/her circumstances.

Table 5-2
Attorney Group by Method and Stage of Adjudication

| | Sample Statistics, Metrocourt, 1967 (percentages) | | | |
| | Lower Court | | Superior Court | |
Status	Public Defender	Private Attorney	Public Defender	Private Attorney
Dismissals	39.4	41.9	3.9	.8
Pleas	51.3	32.4	92.1	91.2
Trials	9.3	25.7	3.9	8.0
Totals	N = 76	N = 74	N = 76	N = 114
	Chi square is significant at .01 level. Raw chi square is 25.30 with 2 df.		Chi square is not significant. Raw chi square is 3.18 with 2 df.	

place differing pressures upon the public defender and privately retained attorney which shape and create differing work styles; this interpretation of the statistics is discussed in the following sections.

Case Closing. Crowded court dockets are reflected in the large case volume handled by the public defender, which places pressure on this attorney to close cases quickly:

You take into consideration their volume in one day. They may represent 60 percent to 70 percent of the calendar. (Judge, Lower Court)

Although statistics have revealed that the level of representation is closer to 50 percent, a large volume of cases is handled by a very few attorneys, leaving the impression of higher caseload per attorney, as the judge in the quotation stated. The operational goal of ease and speed of case adjudication is as relevant for the operation of the office of the public defender as it is for the court itself.

The private attorney, on the other hand, has the potential to work with his client in more depth, over a longer period of time, merely because of less volume and less pressure from an administrative machine:

A private lawyer handles one single case. The public defender may have ten in one day. The private lawyer may be better prepared to discuss more of the facts of the case in depth. (Judge, Superior Court)

A three-month discrepancy exists between the average length of public-defender and private-attorney cases in the Lower Court and a two-month discrepancy in the Superior Court; in both courts the public defender disposes of his cases more quickly than the privately retained attorney.[10] Case volume may influence the speed with which the public defender closes his cases.

Jail or Bail. Table 5-1 reveals that defendants represented by the public defender are more likely to be in jail pending adjudication than defendants represented by the privately retained attorney. Approximately 60 percent of the public defender's clients are jailed during Lower Court adjudication (compared to 27 percent of the private attorney's clients), and 79 percent are jailed during Superior Court adjudication (compared to 42 percent of the private attorney's clients).

These statistics may reflect: (1) the financial criteria a defendant must meet to receive free legal assistance; (2) the varying prior-conviction records of defendants represented by the two attorney groups and the meaning of these records to the court; and (3) differences in offenses handled. The ability to post bail almost by definition excludes the defendant from meeting the regulated poverty standards for acceptance for public defense. It is assumed that a defendant who can afford bail (even if posted by a friend or relative) can afford to pay for the services of a private attorney.

A prior-conviction record brings with it the informal court policy of setting bail (rather than release on one's own recognizance). The public defender is more likely to be defending a client who has a prior record of convictions; approximately 62 percent of the public defender's clients have one or more convictions, while the corresponding statistic is 36 percent for clients of the private attorney.

In a previous chapter it was noted that burglaries and robberies are considered relatively "serious" offenses by court officials; these offenses are overrepresented in the caseload of the public defender and may partially account for the jailed status of the defender's clients. Serious offenses, coupled with defendants with prior-conviction records, most often result in high bail being set by the judge—a particularly formidable problem for the indigent. This leads to a preliminary conclusion that differences in the quality of representation may not be responsible for differences in bail status. Rather, it may be real differences in the offenders and offenses represented by the two attorney groups.

Plea or Trial. There is a statistically significant difference in the method used by the public defender and private attorney to adjudicate cases in the Lower Court; the public defender offers more pleas (51.3 percent of the cases compared with 32.4 percent for the private attorney) and the private attorney adjudicates more often by trial (25.7 percent of the cases compared with 9.3 percent for the public defender). Method of adjudication is similar, however, for cases represented by both attorneys in the Superior Court (Table 5-2). The fact that the public defender's caseload is more crowded in the Lower Court than in the Superior Court may explain some of the difference in method of adjudication found in the two courts for the two attorney groups. The defender's caseload in the Superior Court is less than half of that of his office colleague who is stationed in the Lower Court. Where the public defender's caseload is lighter, office pressure to take a quick plea is not as great.

Similarities in plea-taking between the public defender and private attorney in the Superior Court are also partly related to the private attorney's concern with the client's fee. Misdemeanor trials in the Lower Court are usually held before a one- or three-man bench, a relatively fast occurrence, while felony trials in the Superior Court involve a jury trial. According to one public defender, it doesn't "pay," literally and figuratively, for a private attorney to go to trial in the Superior Court:

A private attorney can't come up here (Superior Court trial section) and make any money. So they take dispositions (pleas). (Public Defender, Superior Court)

Similar sentiments are voiced by a private attorney who frequently appears in the Superior Court:

The fee has a lot to do with plea-taking. For instance, if we've (client and attorney) agreed upon a particular fee and I find that he doesn't come up with it when he's supposed to or gives (me) only a small part to keep (me) going, the tendency is to want to dispose of his case quickly. If you go to trial you'll never get it—especially if he's convicted. (Private Defense Attorney)

Blumberg has noted the recurrent problem of the private attorney fixing a fee and justifying it:[11]

Defense lawyers make sure that even the most obtuse clients know there is a firm connection between fee payment and the zealous exercise of professional expertise, secret knowledge, and organizational "connections" in their behalf. They try to keep their clients at the precise edge of anxiety calculated to encourage prompt payment of fee. . . . By playing upon his client's anxieties and establishing a seemingly causal relationship between the fee and the accused's extrication from his difficulties, the lawyer establishes the necessary groundwork to assure a minimum of haggling over the fee and its eventual payment.

The public defender, on the other hand, is caught up in the demands of the bureaucracy of the public-defender office, rather than in fee demands of the private defense attorney; moving cases is as important for him/her as it is for the prosecutor and judge. Motions, stipulations, hearings, and trials each take time, and time is the least expendable resource available. The pressure of speedy adjudication under which the public defender works is well recognized:

An attorney with time to investigate and give attention to his client does good work. But the public defender is pressured and we know it. He's particularly good in pleas due to volume. (Judge, Lower Court)

One public defender gave the following example of differences between attorney types in handling a particular case:

A cop says "move along" and a kid won't. He's in front of his friends and he's arrested for Disorderly Conduct. The private counsel makes a big deal—histrionics, speeches. We don't have time for that. We have to move the cases. (Public Defender, Lower Court)

Although the greater frequency with which the private attorney goes to trial in the Lower Court offers a partial explanation for the three-month gap in case length between attorneys, it cannot explain the two-month gap in case length in the Superior Court (where trial percentages are similar). Here it appears that the greater work flexibility of the private attorney partially accounts for the time difference. It is operationally more difficult for a public defender who is "stationed" in a court section to maneuver his cases through continued adjournments:

The courts use us as a whipping boy. They let private attorneys adjourn without inquiry—and seem to think we should always be prepared. (Public Defender, Superior Court)
    If you get a tough judge in a part, a private attorney can juggle his case. But we can't—we have too many. (Public Defender, Lower Court)

The private attorney asks for an adjournment with the excuse that he is representing another client in a different court at the same time. The sheer physical presence of the public defender falsely convinces judges that s/he can always be counted on to perform for his/her client. The private attorney will also ask for an adjournment if his client does not show up in court on the stipulated date. Since the greater proportion of defendants represented by public defenders are in jail pending adjudication, clients are always available to the court.

Private attorneys try to prolong the case, hoping the complainant will drop out. The defendant won't show up the first or second call on the calendar. So a bench warrant is sought out, but he shows up in the P.M. He can do it once. Anymore than once and we know he's playing games. He comes in when the cop and complainant leave, hoping they won't come back the next time. (Judge, Lower Court)

The higher "stakes" in the Superior Court, in terms of potential felony dispositions and sentences, reduce the private attorney's readiness to withstand the uncertainties of trial. According to one public defender commenting on the role of private defense, "If he thinks that the defendant can be proved guilty, he must of necessity accept the offer." At stake is the reputation of the defense attorney with his/her current client and future referrals, both of which are related to his/her fee. Although private-attorney cases are not taken on a contingency-fee basis, the disappointed defendant is a difficult party from which to pry owed monies.

It is difficult to discount the role played by the jail status of the public defender's client, and the community status of the client of the private defense attorney, while both have a hearing pending:

The defendant who makes bail and can afford to pay for his attorney's time will delay as much as possible, look for the right judge, approach the arresting officer, and use all the fancy footwork possible. But if the defendant is jailed, he wants to get the whole thing over with. (Judge, Lower Court)

Interviews with defendants undertaken by Casper underscore the "rottenness" of pretrial detention and the strong pressure it places on the defendant to get it over with, to cop out.[12]

In summary, differences in case management between private and public defense appear to be related to the different occupational and organizational contexts within which each works and the differences in offenses and offenders they represent. The public defender is responsive primarily to demands made upon him by the Office of the Public Defender, a large organization with a bureaucratic hierarchy of authority and a concern for efficiency in administration and operation. This attorney works for a regular annual salary and is committed to defending any indigent arraigned in Metrocourt who meets the defined poverty standards. The "practice" of the public defender in Metrocourt is regulated by the practices of the Office of the Public Defender. The clients of this attorney are likely to have committed serious offenses and have prior convictions.

The private attorney, in contrast, is primarily a solo attorney who occasionally works in partnership with one or two other attorneys; both criminal and civil law cases are handled when partnerships exist. This attorney works on a fee basis and is dependent upon case referrals. The success of his practice, which is usually assessed by his financial worth, depends upon client satisfaction. Differences in caseload, work flexibility, and compensation, which are directly related to differences in work contexts, are important variables in explaining case-management differences.

These differences set the stage for understanding the "power" variable which plays an important role in the Bureaucratic Politics Model. The section which follows focuses more directly on this variable and looks into the statistics of differential dispositions and sentences.

Favorable Representation

Research on the public defender undertaken in the early 1960s concluded that indigent defendants were getting inferior representation in court. It was therefore surprising to find many prosecutors and judges in Metrocourt who felt that clients of the public defender received as favorable, if not more favorable, dispositions (i.e., final charge) than clients of the private attorney. The public defender was perceived to have a series of advantages over the private attorney. These advantages were claimed to lie primarily: in an intimate working relationship with the prosecutor and judge . . .

The public defender gets better and more pleas than private counsel because we exert more pressure. We get to know judges on and off the bench. We get to know who to take a plea before; for example, in a rape case, whether it will be a rape or assault or in an assault case, whether it will be seen as a vicious crime or two friends drinking. (Public Defender, Lower Court)

If you're in a court section with the same prosecutor and judge for months you get to know their idiosyncracies. (Public Defender, Superior Court)

. . . in the resources which can be called upon for assistance . . .

If a judge pushes me around, I have the whole strength of the public defender's office behind me and a strong Appeals Bureau. But he might push a private attorney around. (Public Defender, Lower Court)

Public defenders are a power unto themselves and get away with murder. They feel that everyone except them is a shyster. They've been given a position that has proven Frankensteinian for the court. (Judge, Lower Court)

. . . in the sheer volume of cases represented daily. . .

Instead of adjourning a case for a long period of time, I can take out forty writs of *habeas corpus* to every one of a private attorney. (Public Defender, Lower Court)

. . . in the potential to use a caseload to "threaten" the court with trials it can't handle. . .

Public defenders have certain advantages at times because of the case-load . . . they make things difficult in the trial courts. (Private Defense Attorney)

. . . in an ability, due to case volume, to play cases off against each other. . .

Since they (public defenders) have such a large volume to bargain with, they will give a little in Case A and will expect to get a little in Case B. (Private Defense Attorney)

. . . in an ability to jockey cases and "shop around" . . .[13]

We can arrange cases, maneuver them so we can shop around. . . . We get a copy of the judge's assignments. . . . We try to arrange the cases. (Public Defender, Lower Court)

...and in a ready recourse for grievances within the informal court structures ...

I can walk in there anytime (the prosecutor's office) and discuss a case. (Public Defender, Lower Court)

It should be noted that the above statements are perceptions of those interviewed. Many of the same "advantages" are equally attributed to the private attorney who has a relatively large criminal practice (proportionate to the other cases he represents), and who spends a great deal of time in criminal courts. The experienced attorney who is in a daily or weekly work relationship with the prosecutor and judge is said to become fully cognizant of the informal norms of the court. S/he is able to judge-shop and utilize adjournments to a client's advantage. According to some officials, the former prosecuting-attorney-turned-defense has even greater advantages, in terms of receiving "considerations" from prosecutors: the prosecutor might not ask for a bench warrant if the defendant does not show up in court at the appropriate day; the case might be called out of turn or delayed, depending upon the availability of the attorney; the prosecutor will never embarrass the attorney in front of his client; the attorney might receive a "shade of a plea below" the usual norm. The most significant help a defense attorney can be given by a prosecuting attorney, according to the latter, is to have the prosecutor impress the attorney's client with the fact that the attorney knows the prosecutor well, and that s/he is a former prosecutor:

I impress his client with the fact that he's a former prosecutor and I know him. I've done more for him than anything. Now his client thinks he's a buddy of the court. (Prosecuting Attorney, Lower Court)

A distinction is made by legal officials, however, between sentences and dispositions received by the clients of both types of attorneys. Some officials indicated that private defense attorneys receive more favorable sentences for their clients, and that this is directly related to differing occupational demands. The private attorney is judged by his/her clients primarily on the basis of the sentence s/he is able to arrange:

A defense lawyer is only as good as the number of people he gets off, or no one will go to him. Defense counsel doesn't work in a vacuum. How long would ... (names a defense attorney) last if he didn't get his clients out. These boys talk in jail. (Prosecuting Attorney, Lower Court)

Alschuler finds that defendants only care about when they will "hit the streets."[14] Case referrals depend largely on client satisfaction. It is known by court officials that "the private attorney is more interested in the sentence than in the plea" (Judge, Lower Court). Invariably the client asks, "Will I have to do time?" or "What happens if I plead guilty to...?" Accordingly, it is considered wise for a private defense attorney with a regular criminal-court practice to try to "hook up" with a judge (i.e., get to know him on and off the bench and try to arrange cases so that his client appears before the judge for sentencing) and to become familiar with the court's informal norms.

The question remaining is whether the perceptions of legal officials about the results of organizational and occupational demands and needs are correct: that is, whether they result in different case outcomes for the clients of the public and private defense attorneys. The section which follows is concerned with whether differences in "favorableness" of dispositions and sentences exist for cases represented by the public defender and the private attorney, and how such differences might be explained or interpreted.

Dispositions. Favorableness of disposition was operationalized as a continuum of three possible adjudicatory alternatives: dismissal of charge, finding of a misdemeanor, finding of a felony. According to Table 5-3, *the relationship between favorable case disposition and attorney representation is not statistically significant either in the Lower Court or Superior Court.* However, the relationship in the Lower Court approaches significance (.08 level of probability) with clients of private attorneys receiving more favorable dispositions (55.4 percent of the cases are dismissed or acquitted) than those of public defenders (40.8 percent of the cases are dismissed or acquitted).

Further analysis is needed, however, before accepting the lack of an association as conclusive. For example, a statistically significant relationship might exist under specified conditions: since the public defender and private attorney represent cases which differ markedly, it may be these differences which are disguising a significant relationship. Thus, favorable disposition and attorney type might be related when offense category is held constant. To look

Table 5-3
Disposition of Attorney Group, Lower and Superior Courts

	Sample Statistics, Metrocourt, 1967 (percentages)			
	Lower Court		Superior Court	
Disposition	Public Defender	Private Attorney	Public Defender	Private Attorney
Dismissal	40.8	55.4	7.8	6.0
Misdemeanor	59.5	44.6	31.2	40.5
Felony	–	–	61.0	53.4
Total	N = 76	N = 74	N = 77	N = 116
	Chi square is not significant. Raw chi square is 3.23 with 1 df.		Chi square is not significant. Raw chi square is 1.84 with 2 df.	

into the possibility of important specifying conditions, case, defendant, and case-management variables were used to explore the original lack of relationship found in Table 5-4.

When prior-conviction record was used as a third variable (hypothesizing that prior record is related to disposition and that defendants represented by public defense have longer conviction records), it does not alter the original nonsignificant relationship (Appendix, Table A-1). Race of defendant could not be held constant, since it is only recorded for cases reaching the Superior Court. The small number of females in the Lower Court sample made it difficult to examine sex of defendant as an explanatory variable.

The large proportion of assault cases adjudicated in the Lower Court excluded consideration of any but this offense category as a third variable. When the relationship between favorable disposition and attorney group was reexamined for the offense of assault, it again remained nonsignificant (Appendix, Table A-2). In other words, regardless of whether a defendant charged with felonious assault was represented by a public defender or private attorney, "favorableness" of disposition did not differ significantly in the Lower Court.

Attorney differences in case management (e.g., method of disposition, time interval of case adjudication) are intervening variables which could bear some relation to favorableness of case disposition. The statistical procedure for testing whether an intervening variable interprets a relationship is identical to that of whether an antecedent variable (e.g., prior-conviction record) explains a relationship. For example, the earlier a case is adjudicated (closed), the less favorable may be the disposition. This would be one attempt to delineate a condition under which the original relationship is significant.

Using "adjudication interval" and "method of disposition" as potentially

Table 5-4
Sentence by Attorney Group, Lower and Superior Courts

	Sample Statistics, Metrocourt, 1967 (percentages)			
	Lower Court		Superior Court	
Sentence	Public Defender	Private Attorney	Public Defender	Private Attorney
Nonconfinement	53.6	66.7	29.3	54.8
One year confinement or less	46.4	33.3	17.3	11.3
One year confinement or more	—	—	53.4	33.9
Total	N = 69	N = 66	N = 75	N = 115
	Chi square is not significant. Raw chi square is 2.39 with 1 df.		Chi square is significant at .01 level. Raw chi square is 11.5 with 2 df.	

intervening and interpreting third variables, the original relationship between favorable disposition and attorney type in the Lower Court remains nonsignificant (Appendix, Tables A-3, A-4). When the nonsignificant relationship between attorney and disposition in the Superior Court is tested against a variety of third variables (Appendixe, Tables A-5 to A-8), the relationship finally takes on significance for the defendant with no prior-conviction record, suggesting that *clients of the public defender who have no prior record, and whose cases reach the Superior Court, receive more favorable dispositions than do similar clients of the private attorney.*

To summarize, it was originally found that the relationship between favorable disposition and attorney representation was *not* statistically significant. Case, defendant, and management variables were used to reexamine the original relationship in an attempt to explain or interpret the original relationships in the Lower and Superior Courts. The original relationship remained unchanged under almost every condition.[15] This leads to the conclusion that those legal officials who perceive the public defender to have few advantages in court are operating on faulty perceptions. On the basis of the data analyzed, *clients of the public defender and private attorneys receive similar dispositions in the courts,* with the exception of the first offender in the Superior Court. Such statistical findings lend credence to the general conclusion that *organizational priorities and informal norms, which are known and agreed upon by court subgroups, override perceived dispositional "advantages" for either defense attorney groups.*[16]

In the terms of the Bureaucratic Politics Model and the previous discussion, bargaining advantages which are attributed to each attorney group by court officials appear to cancel each other out when favorableness of disposition is viewed as a potential resultant of such advantages. Defendants represented by both public defender or private defense attorneys receive dispositions in both courts which cannot be distinguished on the basis of a test of statistical significance.

Sentences. Favorableness of sentences was operationalized as a continuum of three possible sentencing alternatives—nonconfinement, confinement of less than one year, confinement of more than one year. According to Table 5-4, there is a statistically significant difference between sentence and attorney representation in the Superior Court; inspection of the table reveals that *defendants represented in the Superior Court by the private attorney receive more favorable sentences than do defendants represented by the public defender.* The relationship, however, is not statistically significant for the Lower Court sample.

Just as test variables were used to help clarify the disposition/attorney relationship, the sentencing/attorney relationship can be dissected in a similar manner. According to the informal working code of the court and data discussed in Chapter 4, it would be expected that defendants with long prior-conviction records are sentenced less favorably regardless of the representing attorney. If private attorneys represent defendants with such records, the above relationship might be explained. However, when prior-conviction record of defendant was held constant, the original significant relationship between favorableness of sentence and private attorney remained for those defendants with no or one previous conviction who reached disposition in the Superior Court (Appendix, Tables A-9, A-10). The relationship disappeared for defendants with two or more convictions. Since subdividing a sample almost inevitably leads to lowered statistical significance levels (using the chi square test), the fact that a statistically significant relationship is maintained is all the more important.[17] It can be concluded that *defendants with a relatively good prior record (none or one prior conviction) are sentenced more favorably when represented by the private attorney;* there is no difference in sentencing for those defendants with two or more previous convictions, irrespective of attorney representation. Using race of defendant as a potential explanatory variable, it was found that the *relationship between favorableness of sentence and attorney type continues to be statistically significant for nonwhite defendants represented by a private defense attorney* (Appendix, Table A-11). *The sentencing/attorney relationship also maintains its statistical significance for males represented by private defense* (Appendix, Table A-12).

A relatively similar distribution of cases represented by public defenders private attorneys in this court allowed a closer look at the relationship between favorableness of sentence and attorney type for the offense categories of assault, drug abuse, and robbery (Appendix, Table A-13). When offense was held constant, the statistical significance of the original relation remained only for the offense of assault; *clients represented by private attorneys who are charged with assault, and whose cases reach adjudication in the Superior Court, received better sentences than similar cases represented by the public defender.* However, it seems that whether a favorable sentence is received by clients of private defense varies by offense category.

To summarize, the sample statistics suggested that *the relation between favorableness of sentence and representation by a private attorney in the Superior Court is maintained for defendants with one or no prior conviction record, defendants who are nonwhite, defendants who are male, and defendants who are charged with the offense of assault; in other words, the overwhelming majority of defendants in Metrocourt.*[18]

Do the case-management techniques of the attorney groups differ enough from each other so that case-management variables account for the relationship? Utilizing "adjudicatory interval" and "method of disposition" as potentially interpreting third variables, the original relationship remains generally unchanged (Appendix, Table A-9). It appears that the privately retained defense attorney, judged successful by his clients on a standard of favorable sentences, does in fact "out-bargain" the public defender in Superior Court. When the relationship between sentence and attorney type was reexamined in light of cases closed by a plea of guilty (i.e., the number of cases dismissed and tried were too small for analysis) the statistical significance of the sentencing/attorney type relation for those cases closed by the plea of guilty remained (Appendix, Table A-14).

Do sentencing differences exist between attorney groups in the Lower Court as they do in the Superior Court? On the basis of the qualitative material collected one might speculate that differences in the volume of cases between courts make the Lower Court more of an "assembly-line" operation, a term used by many court officials to describe the workings of this court. Sheer numbers and the need to adjudicate quickly mitigate against preferential treatment, or, in other words, "dispose" the court to favorable case treatment across the board merely to reduce the pressure of numbers. Since "stakes" are also lower in this court (that is, the sentencing range available to the judge is smaller and the sentences themselves are relatively minor when compared with those possible in the Superior Court), there may be less need for the private attorney to use, or use up, his/her advantages at this level of adjudication.

Just as the meaning of the nonsignificant disposition/attorney relationship in the Lower Court and Superior Court was explored, defendant-characteristics (prior-conviction record, sex), offense-category (assault), and case-management (interval and method of disposition) variables were used as test factors for the lack of relationship between sentence and attorney in the Lower Court. Significance in the original relationship was uncovered only for the private attorney who closes cases within three months (Appendix, Table A-15). That is, *private attorneys who close quickly in the Lower Court receive better sentences for their clients than do public defenders.*

Notes

1. Edgar and Jean Cahn, "The War on Poverty: A Civilian Perspective," *Yale Law Journal,* 73, July 1964, 1317-51. J. Carlin and J. Howard, "Legal Representation and Class Justice," *U.C.L.A. Law Review,* 12, Rochester: Lawyers Cooperative Publishing Company, 1951. *Equal Justice for the Accused,* Special Committee for the Association of the Bar of the City of New York and the National Legal Aid Defender Association. New York: Doubleday and Company, 1957. R. Seegal, "Some Procedural and Strategic Inequities in Defending the Indigent," *American Bar Association Journal,* 51, 1965, 1165-82.

2. Laura Banfield and C. David Anderson, "Continuances in the Cook County Criminal Courts," *University of Chicago Law Review,* 35, 1967-68, 259-316. S. Zamsky, "Effects of Bail and Other Pre-Trial Procedures on Outcome, Plea and Speedy Trial" (University of Oregon Law School). Stephen R. Bing and Stephen Rosenfeld, *The Quality of Justice.* Boston: Lawyer's Committee for Civil Rights Under Law, 1970.

3. L. Katz et. al., *Justice is the Crime: Pretrial Delay in Felony Cases.* Washington, D.C.: Report to the National Institute of Law Enforcement and Criminal Justice on the LEAA, 1971. J. Feinman, "Effective Counsel and Criminal Justice: A Statistical Study of Defense Counsel in the Criminal Courts of the District of Columbia," February 1971 (Unpublished paper, School of Government and Public Administration, The American University). G. Smith, *A Statistical Analysis of Public Defender Activities,* Ohio State University Research Foundation, June 1970. Jean Taylor et. al., "Analysis of Defense Counsel in the Processing of Felony Defendants in San Diego, California," *Denver Law Journal,* 49, 1972, 233-75.

4. Dallin Oaks and Warren Lehman, "Lawyers for the Poor," *Transaction,* July-August, 1967, 22-29. See also Lee Silverstein, *Defense of the Poor.* Chicago: American Bar Foundation, 1965.

5. Graham T. Allison, *Essence of Decision: Explaining the Cuban Missile Crisis.* Boston: Little, Brown and Company, 1971, pp. 162, 170, 171. Reprinted by permission.

6. Warner Shilling, "The Politics of National Defense: Fiscal 1950," in W. Schilling, P. Hammond, and G. Snyder, *Strategy, Politics, and Defense Budgets.* New York: Columbia University Press, 1962.

7. Roger Hilsman, *To Move A Nation.* New York: Dell Publishing, 1967.

8. Allison, op. cit. These propositions summarize Allison's position.

9. The decision to look within the defense-attorney subgroup, instead of within prosecutorial or judicial groups, was made partly to shed light on the arguments mentioned earlier in this chapter and partly because the information on this group was more readily available in case records.

10. Banfield and Anderson, op. cit., have also found that the proportion of guilty dispositions decreases as the number of court appearances increases, and that private attorneys take longer than public defenders to close cases.

11. Abraham Blumberg, *Criminal Justice.* Chicago: Quadrangle Books, 1967, p. 111. Copyright 1967 by Abraham S. Blumberg, First New Viewpoints Edition published 1974 by Franklin Watts, Inc. Used by permission.

12. Jonathan D. Casper, *American Criminal Justice: The Defendant's Perspective.* Englewood Cliffs, New Jersey: Prentice-Hall, Inc., 1972, p. 16. Reprinted by permission of Prentice-Hall, Inc., Englewood Cliffs, New Jersey.

13. This is disputed by some public defenders who claim a greater rigidity in case prosecution due to the judges' assumption that the defender, as full-time court-affiliated defense, should always be prepared.

14. Albert W. Alschuler, "The Prosecutor's Role in Plea Bargaining," *University of Chicago Law Review,* 36, 1968-69, 50-111.

15. Jean Taylor, op. cit., reports similar findings: i.e., differences in conviction rates for cases represented by legal aid and private attorney disappear when subjected to third variable exploration. However, the author speculates that the use of continuances and motions, to lengthen the adjudicatory

procedures (utilized primarily by private attorneys) may be related to differences initially found in conviction rates.

16. By accepting the relationship between defense attorney group and case disposition as having no statistical significance, we run the risk of rejecting a true relationship. However, the statistical use of antecedent and intermediary variables, coupled with our interview and observational materials, lead us to conclude that the lack of association is correct.

17. These tables are addressed to the question of the significance of the relationship, recognizing that there is a difference between the concepts of significance and magnitude (or strength). An assessment of the latter would call for tests measuring the strength of association, such as the Theta, Cramer's V, or Pearson's C. Without the use of these tests, questions have been limited to: Does a statistically significant difference exist between type of attorney and the variable(s) of concern? There is no descriptive measure applied to summarize the relationship in such a manner that several can be compared and a conclusion reached as to which is the strongest.

18. Sample size is too small to consider the simultaneous interaction of all of the above variables.

6

Implications for Criminal Justice Research

The preceding chapters attempted to dissect the adjudication of felony cases in one urban court from several perspectives. Throughout, it was assumed that court statistics result from the varying objectives, demands, and constraints under which the court and its authorized officials work. The adjudication process was viewed as an assembly line, a machine which begins with those arrested as its raw material and ends with the exonerated or guilty as its product:[1]

Between arrest and disposition are a series of points on the assembly line: the preliminary hearing, the stay in jail awaiting trial, the bargaining about a "deal" (e.g., a reduction of charges in exchange for a guilty plea), the cop-out (plea of guilty), the sentencing day. The machine has some quality controls, and some of the objects are "rejected" and thrown off the assembly line at various stages, as charges are dropped, witnesses don't show up, imperfections in the state's case emerge. But the machine grinds on, processing its materials and turning over cases. The crucial aspects of the process—the bargaining, the quality of legal representation . . . are determined by a necessity to keep the system functioning, to ensure that it does not collapse under the weight of its own work.

The chapter which follows summarizes the data and findings of this volume and points out areas for future research.

The Models

Each of the three frames of reference discussed—the Rational Actor Model, the Organizational Process Model, the Bureaucratic Politics Model—distinguishes different features as important for explaining felony adjudication. Each attempts to explain certain features of the court in operation which are relevant for understanding case processing and outcome. Each, however, has insufficient explanatory power without consideration of the others.

The Rational Actor Model: Administrative Efficiency

The Rational Actor Model, used in Chapter 3 to interpret guilty-plea and case-screening statistics, views case processing as purposeful acts of legal officials whose primary operational goal is to maximize the administrative efficiency of the criminal courts. Why are both pleas of guilty and case dismissals used by the court as major methods of adjudication? To explain these statistics, the Rational Actor Model considers the court's strategic calculus: the problem posed by a high case volume/low court resource imbalance, relevant court objectives, and potential alternatives and their consequences. In this calculus, trials are viewed as court failures: failures to negotiate "terms" among prosecution, defense, and bench, which limit the achievement of administrative efficiency.

The statistical data indicate that the majority of cases found guilty are adjudicated by the mechanism of pleading guilty. In the Lower Court, the guilty plea accounts for 43 percent of all adjudications (including dismissals and acquittals) and 73 percent of those cases adjudicated guilty; in the Superior Court the statistics are 92 percent and 94 percent, respectively.

Several reasons may explain why the guilty plea is useful for the continued operational viability of the court: speed of adjudication, ease of operations, limited case return, and flexibility in case management. The screening out of felony cases at differing stages of adjudication was also considered, with particular attention to the dismissal statistic. This statistic, while possibly reflecting defendant innocence or prosecutorial lack of evidence, most probably reflects management procedures instituted by the criminal court; that is, a conscious decision on the part of the court and prosecutor whether or not to use available mechanisms, such as the adjournment, the warrant, or reinvestigation, to abet or avoid a case dismissal.

The probability that a particular method of adjudication will be used appears to be offense-specific. Although the charges of assault, larceny, and burglary comprise more than 60 percent of the felonies arraigned in Metrocourt, they comprise only 30 percent of those cases reaching adjudication in the Superior Court. The offenses of drug abuse, robbery, and homicide are overrepresented in the Superior Court, in relation to their proportions of the total number of cases. In an efficiency calculus only a limited number of cases can be given full treatment. Which cases these will be is best explained through another model, the Organizational Process Model.

The Organizational Process Model: Informal Agreements

The Rational Actor Model's implication that "monoliths perform large actions for large reasons," needs to be balanced by an appreciation of the "innumerable and often conflicting smaller actions by individuals of bureaucratic organizations in the service of a variety of only partially compatible conceptions. . . ."[2] What the Rational Actor Model characterizes as "acts" or "choices," the Organizational Process Model views as "outputs" of organizations functioning according to regular channels of behavior. The common orientation and informal agreements shared by legal officials regarding offense dispositions serve the purpose of simplifying decision-making and limiting case outcome uncertainties, and can be viewed as the court's operationalization of those negotiated constraints which emerge within an organization. Socialization for prosecution, defense, and bench which takes place within each respective subgroup, combined with informal between-group interactions both within and without the court setting, serves to teach and legitimize informal court norms.

Disposition statistics can be understood using this model. For example, while a large proportion of assault cases are dismissed in the Lower Court and few receive felony dispositions in the Superior Court, a relatively large proportion of robbery cases not only reach adjudication in the Superior Court, but are adjudicated as felonies. Legal evidence does not seem to be the determining factor for differing dispositional outcomes, but rather an informal consensus on case assessment which is institutionalized as typical dispositions. The data indicate that a shared normative system on case dispositions exists which overrides partisan group interests of judge, prosecutor, and defense attorney. This shared system of "normal" case dispositions has at its core the agreement of legal officials on case seriousness. A determination of seriousness is based on the perceptions of legal officials concerning the potential for violence and the tolerance level of the relevant community.

"Normal" sentences, however, were not discovered. It was suggested that sentencing may be one area in which differences in group or individual interests and constraints may supersede informal subgroup agreements.

The Bureaucratic Politics Model: Bargaining Advantages

The third model, the Bureaucratic Politics Model, focuses on the politics of court operation, and the different interests of legal officials. Decision-making in court is understood, according to this model, neither as choices nor as outputs. Rather, case adjudication is viewed as a resultant of various bargaining games among legal officials in court. The Bureaucratic Politics Model is helpful in interpreting the sentencing differences found in the data between defendants represented by public defenders and those represented by privately retained attorneys; clients represented by private defense in the Superior Court receive more favorable sentences. The statistical data imply that sentencing decisions, more than dispositional decisions, are the result of bargaining advantages differentially distributed among defense-attorney groups.

The discussion of differing roles of the public defender and privately retained attorney in case management and outcome concluded that public defenders close their cases faster and offer more guilty pleas. However, contrary to conclusions of some prior research, they receive dispositions for their clients which are similar to those received by clients of the private attorney. The private attorney does do "better" for the first offender and the individual charged with assault, and for clients whose cases reach disposition and sentencing in the Superior Court. A variety of structural variables, organizational context, fee structure, and performance goals which differ for both attorney groups, may influence case management and outcome. The public defender, because of his organizational affiliation, prescribed annual salary, and intraoffice administrative criteria for successful performance does not have the incentives that the private attorney has in case representation. The public defender is responsive to the demands of the court, while the private attorney, working alone, on a fee basis, with his client as his judge, is particularly responsive to the sentencing demands of his/her client. Sentences, more than convictions, are the success criteria for most defendants.

Additional Research

The 1960s witnessed an increasing number of studies in the area of criminal justice. Whether these studies focused on law enforcement, the courts, or corrections, each necessarily highlighted some data, explanations, and issues at the expense of others. The present study is no exception, although a variety of data were introduced and three models of analysis were distinguished which are relevant for data interpretation. The next question to consider, then, is which issues or data require further research. The focus of the response is on the models discussed, rather than branching into areas which are important, such as the impact of the external environment on court behavior, but tangential to the concerns of this volume.

Using the propositions of the Rational Actor Model, plea bargaining and case screening were shown to be useful and expedient for all legal agents in Metrocourt. The given operating conditions, however, were an imbalance between caseload and resources. What might have happened if this imbalance did not exist? Or if the amount of resources outstripped the number of defendants? Around what objective(s) would the legal actors agree to work, if any? Researchers would do well to uncover, and federal agencies to fund, a criminal-justice system which did *not* resemble the overcrowded ones of many large and medium-sized cities. Given a new environment, what goal(s) might be substituted for that of operational survival? What would new goals mean for case-processing statistics? In which ways would new concerns, activities, and decisions affect the defendant? Which of the auxiliary institutions and programs, such as pretrial screening, jails, or corrections, would be impacted upon? In short, keeping the assumptions of the model but altering some of the ground rules would be a worthwhile research enterprise as well as a practical lesson in American justice.

During the decade since the 1967 Crime Commission report, a great deal of attention has been given to the questions of whether a criminal-justice system exists and, if it does not, whether it is a desirable goal to work toward. Discussion surrounds mechanisms which attempt to link system parts as well as the differing objectives toward which these parts often work. While legal officials who function daily on an operational level point to cracks in the system, federal, state, and local governments are busy attempting to fill some of those cracks with funds and special projects. The data presented in this volume suggest that there is more of a criminal-justice system in operation in the criminal court than is generally acknowledged. Its existence, however, is least understood by looking into formal objectives and mechanistic linkages. Rather, its existence can be documented through an operational understanding of such concepts as consensus, dependency, and perceptions.

The Organization Process Model focuses attention on the informal norms which arise when individuals in an organization work closely over periods of time. The data presented, however, were only a small indication of the consensus which exists among subgroups with apparently differing objectives. Other criminal courts should be researched to consider the important stereotypes in depth: Does consensus exist among court subgroups? What is the nature and extent of that consensus? Which subgroups are in most agreement? What conditions foster and impede the development of consensus? What are the consequences of consenses for differing defendants? For the criminal justice system? In this latter regard, it would be appropriate to compare consensus which exists among court personnel with attitudes of police and corrections. A full understanding of the origin, nature, and consequences of consensus, or a lack thereof, among court and other legal actors is probably a necessary step for any implementation of desired system change to be successful.

Distinct from the concept of consensus is that of dependency. It is typical in legalistic tracts to assume independence of function on the part of legal subgroups, an independence which is an integral part of the criminal-justice system. The data suggest, however, that for a variety of reasons, dependencies do exist among prosecution, defense, and bench. The nature of these dependencies, and their consequences for case processing and outcome, should be more fully researched. Additional components might be considered, such as probation and the police. A study of court operations from the perspective of the role played by the defendant might most poignantly highlight the intricate network of dependencies which exist in court.

The third concept inviting study, that of perception, was illuminated by data which reveal the large degree to which decisions on case worth, such as those made by prosecutors, are based on what legal actors perceive to be community tolerance of deviance. Are some or all of these perceptions accurate? In which areas, and on what topics, do perceptions guide legal decisions? How similar are the perceptions of differing legal subgroups? An essential study would research the perceptions and case decisions of legal actors in relation to existing statutes covering case adjudication.

The concept of power differentials has dominated the prior decade of academic teachings as well as activist politics. Both groups point out, as does Chapter 5 in this volume, that power differentials result in institutionalized inequality. The inequalities are not maliciously planned, however, to discriminate against a particular group. Rather, they result from power differentials—from individual attributes to work environments—which have been heretofore taken for granted. While sentencing differentials may not be explainable by differences in the conduct of those convicted, neither do they, as labeling theory suggests, represent prejudices of the sentencers.

The Bureaucratic Politics Model asks the researcher to be more sensitive to inter- and intragroup power differentials. An essential "first question" is to discover, for any individual criminal-justice system, where the power resides for different activities and decisions. This volume has shown that power in sentencing favors the private defense attorney over the public defense attorney. Which decisions are made through power plays involving the judge and probation staff, or different levels of the prosecutorial hierarchy, which eventually influence the fortunes of the defendant? The ability to pinpoint differentials and provide indications for their measurement would lead to predictive models in decision-making.

Notes

1. Jonathan D. Casper, *American Criminal Justice: The Defendant's Perspective.* Englewood Cliffs, New Jersey: Prentice Hall, Inc., 1972, p. 2. Reprinted by permission of Prentice-Hall, Inc., Englewood Cliffs, New Jersey.

2. Graham Allison, *Essence of Decision: Explaining the Cuban Missile Crisis.* Boston: Little, Brown, & Co., 1971, pp. 5-6. Reprinted by permission.

Appendix

Table A-1

Favorableness of Disposition by Attorney Group and Prior-Conviction Record of Defendant in the Lower Court

Disposition	% No Prior Record		% One Conviction		% Two Convictions +	
	Legal Aid	Private	Legal Aid	Private	Legal Aid	Private
Dismissal	56.5 (13)	65.0 (26)	45.5 (5)	37.5 (3)	29.6 (8)	8.6 (4)
Misdemeanor	43.5 (10)	35.0 (14)	54.5 (6)	62.5 (5)	70.4 (19)	71.4 (1)
	Chi square is not significant. Raw chi square is 1.018 with 1 df.		Fishers Exact Test is not significant at .550.		Chi square is not significant. Raw chi square is .215 with 1 df.	

Table A-2

Favorableness of Disposition by Attorney Group for the Offense of Assault in the Lower Court

Disposition	% Legal Aid	% Private
Dismissal	60.0 (21)	60.0 (24)
Misdemeanor	40.0 (14)	40.0 (16)
Total	(35)	(40)

Chi square is not significant. Raw chi square is 0.

Table A-3

Favorableness of Disposition by Attorney Group and Length of Interval between Arraignment and Disposition in the Lower Court

	Adjudication Interval					
	% Within 3 Months		% 3-7 Months		% 7 Months +	
Disposition	Legal Aid	Private	Legal Aid	Private	Legal Aid	Private
Dismissal	27.8 (13)	40.5 (9)	66.7 (12)	59.1 (13)	62.5 (5)	64.5 (20)
Misdemeanor	72.2 (35)	59.5 (11)	33.3 (6)	40.9 (9)	37.5 (3)	35.5 (11)
Total	(48)	(20)	(18)	(22)	(8)	(31)
	Chi square is not significant. Raw chi square is 2.01 with 1 df.		Chi square is not significant. Raw chi square is .21 with 1 df.		Chi square is not significant. Raw chi square is .03 with 1 df.	

Table A-4

Favorableness of Disposition by Attorney Group and Method of Disposition in the Lower Court

Disposition	% Dismissal		% Pleas		% Trial	
	Legal Aid	Private	Legal Aid	Private	Legal Aid	Private
Dismissal	100.0 (30)	100.0 (31)	– –	– –	14.3 (1)	52.6 (10)
Misdemeanor	– –	– –	100.0 (39)	100.0 (24)	85.7 (6)	47.7 (9)
Total	(30)	(31)	(39)	(24)	(7)	(19)

Chi square (corrected) is not significant. Raw chi square is 1.71 with 1 df.

Table A-5

Favorableness of Disposition by Attorney Group and Prior-Conviction Record of Defendant in the Superior Court

Disposition	% No Prior Record		% One Conviction		% Two Convictions +	
	Legal Aid	Private	Legal Aid	Private	Legal Aid	Private
Dismissal	12.9 (4)	– –	– –	– –	– –	13.3 (4)
Misdemeanor	25.8 (8)	50.0 (32)	35.7 (5)	70.0 (7)	37.0 (10)	26.7 (8)
Felony	61.3 (19)	50.0 (32)	64.3 (9)	30.0 (3)	63.0 (17)	60.0 (18)
Total	(31)	(64)	(14)	(10)	(27)	(30)

| Chi square is significant at .01 level. Raw chi square is 11.657 with 2 df. | Chi square (corrected) is not significant. Corrected chi square is 1.54 with 2 df. | Chi square is not significant. Raw chi square is 4.12 with 2 df. |

Table A-6
Favorableness of Disposition by Attorney Group for Selected Offenses in the Superior Court

Disposition	% Assault		% Burglary	
	Legal Aid	Private	Legal Aid	Private
Dismissal	9.1 (1)	6.7 (1)	— —	14.3 (1)
Misdemeanor	45.5 (5)	53.3 (8)	22.2 (2)	— —
Felony	45.5 (5)	40.0 (6)	77.8 (7)	85.7 (6)
Total	(11)	(15)	(9)	(7)

Chi square is not significant.
Raw chi square is .17 with
2 df.

Disposition	% Drug Abuse		% Robbery	
	Legal Aid	Private	Legal Aid	Private
Dismissal	10.5 (2)	— —	13.6 (3)	6.3 (1)
Misdemeanor	47.4 (9)	54.3 (19)	— —	6.3 (1)
Felony	42.1 (8)	45.7 (16)	86.4 (19)	87.5 (14)
Total	(19)	(35)	(22)	(16)

Table A-7
Favorableness of Disposition by Attorney Group and Length of Interval between Arraignment and Disposition in the Superior Court

Disposition	Adjudication Interval					
	% Within 3 Months		% 3-7 Months		% 7 Months +	
	Legal Aid	Private	Legal Aid	Private	Legal Aid	Private
Dismissal	2.8 (1)	3.0 (1)	9.4 (3)	1.9 (1)	25.0 (2)	16.7 (5)
Misdemeanor	30.6 (11)	42.4 (14)	31.3 (10)	48.1 (25)	37.5 (3)	26.7 (8)
Felony	66.7 (24)	54.5 (18)	59.4 (19)	50.0 (26)	37.5 (3)	56.7 (17)
Total	(36)	(33)	(32)	(52)	(8)	(30)

Chi square is not significant. Raw chi square is 1.08 with 2 df.	Chi square is not significant. Raw chi square is 3.88 with 2 df.	Chi square is not significant. Raw chi square is .93 with 2 df.

Table A-8

Favorableness of Disposition by Attorney Group and Race of Defendant in the Superior Court

	% Nonwhite		% White	
Disposition	Legal Aid	Private	Legal Aid	Private
Dismissal	3.3 (2)	1.4 (1)	– –	5.9 (2)
Misdemeanor	30.0 (18)	34.2 (25)	50.0 (4)	52.9 (18)
Felony	66.7 (40)	64.4 (47)	50.0 (4)	41.2 (14)
Total	(60)	(73)	(8)	(34)
	Chi square is not significant. Raw chi square is .66 with 2 df.		Chi square is not significant. Raw chi square is .59 with 2 df.	

Table A-9

Favorableness of Sentence by Attorney Group and Prior-Conviction Record of Defendant in the Lower Court

	% No Prior Record		% One Conviction		% Two Convictions +	
Sentence	Legal Aid	Private	Legal Aid	Private	Legal Aid	Private
Nonconfinement	75.0 (18)	80.0 (28)	66.7 (6)	87.5 (7)	37.0 (10)	23.1 (3)
One year confinement or less	25.0 (6)	20.0 (7)	33.3 (3)	12.5 (1)	63.0 (17)	76.9 (10)
Total	(24)	(35)	(9)	(8)	(27)	(13)
	Chi square is not significant. Corrected chi square is .018 with 1 df.		Fishers Exact Test is not significant at .335.		Chi square is not significant. Corrected chi square is .273 with 1 df.	

Table A-10

Sentence by Attorney Group and Prior-Conviction Record of Defendant in the Superior Court

	No Prior Record		*One Conviction*		*Two Convictions*	
	Legal Aid	*Private*	*Legal Aid*	*Private*	*Legal Aid*	*Private*
Nonconfinement	41.4	65.6	7.1	60.2	18.5	25.0
One year confinement or less	17.2	4.7	14.3	20.0	18.5	17.9
One year confinement or more	41.4	29.7	78.6	20.0	63.0	57.1
Total	(N = 29)	(N = 64)	(N = 14)	(N = 10)	(N = 27)	(N = 28)
	Chi square is significant at .05. Raw chi square is 6.49 with 2 df.		Chi square is significant at .01. Raw chi square is 9.39 with 2 df.		Chi square is not significant. Raw chi square is .33 with 2 df.	

Sample Statistics, 1967, Metrocourt (percentages)

Table A-11

Sentence by Attorney Group and Race of Defendant in the Superior Court

Sample Statistics, 1967, Metrocourt (percentages)

	Nonwhite		*White*	
Sentence	*Legal Aid*	*Private*	*Legal Aid*	*Private*
Nonconfinement	23.3	43.1	50.0	63.6
One year confinement or less	18.3	8.3	12.5	9.1
One year confinement or more	58.3	48.6	37.5	27.3
Total	(N = 60)	(N = 72)	(N = 8)	(N = 33)
	Chi square is significant at .05. Raw chi square is 6.83 with 2 df.		Chi square is not significant. Raw chi square is .503 with 2 df.	

Table A-12
Sentence by Attorney Group and Sex of Defendant in the Superior Court

| | Male | | Female | |
Sentence	Legal Aid	Private	Legal Aid	Private
Nonconfinement	23.2	49.0	80.0	64.3
One year confinement or less	18.8	11.2	–	–
One year confinement or more	58.0	39.8	20.0	35.7
Total	(N = 69)	(N = 98)	(N = 5)	(N = 14)

Sample Statistics, 1967, Metrocourt (percentages)

Chi square is significant at .01. Raw chi square is 11.48 with 2 df.

Fishers Exact Test is nonsignificant at .4796.

Table A-13
Sentence by Attorney Group and Selected Offense in the Superior Court

| | Assault | | Drug Abuse | | Robbery | |
Sentence	Legal Aid	Private	Legal Aid	Private	Legal Aid	Private
Nonconfinement	36.5	73.3	26.3	47.2	12.5	35.3
One year confinement or less	36.5	6.7	21.0	13.9	16.7	11.8
One year confinement or more	27.0	20.0	52.7	38.9	70.8	52.9
Total	(N = 11)	(N = 15)	(N = 19)	(N = 36)	(N = 24)	(N = 17)

Sample Statistics, 1967, Metrocourt (percentages)

Chi square is significant at .05. Raw chi is 6.02 with 2 df.

Chi square is not significant. Raw chi square is 2.28 with 2 df.

Chi square is not significant. Raw chi square is 3.88 with 2 df.

Table A-14

Sentence by Attorney Type and Plea of Guilty in the Superior Court

Sample Statistics, 1967, Metrocourt (percentages)

	Plea of Guilty	
Sentence	*Legal Aid*	*Private*
Nonconfinement	22.9	50.5
One year confinement or less	18.6	10.7
One year confinement or more	58.6	38.8
Total	(N = 70)	(N = 103)

Chi square is significant at .01. Raw chi square is 12.17 with 2 df.

Table A-15

Sentence by Attorney Type and Interval between Arraignment and Disposition in the Superior Court

Sample Statistics, 1967, Metrocourt (percentages)

	Within Three Months		Three-Seven Months		Seven Months +	
Sentence	*Legal Aid*	*Private*	*Legal Aid*	*Private*	*Legal Aid*	*Private*
Nonconfinement	30.6	54.5	16.7	52.9	50.0 (4)	46.7
One year confinement or less	11.1	12.1	20.0	7.8	37.5 (3)	10.7
One year confinement or more	58.3	33.3	63.1	39.2	12.5 (1)	42.6
Total	(N = 36)	(N = 33)	(N = 30)	(N = 51)	(N = 9)	(N = 28)
	Chi square is not significant. Raw chi square is 4.69 with 2 df.		Chi square is significant at .01. Raw chi square is 10.85 with 2 df.		Chi square is not significant. Raw chi square is 4.61 with 2 df.	

Index

Index

About the Author

Roberta Rovner-Pieczenik received the Ph.D. in sociology from New York University. Her professional background includes university-level teaching, administration, research and evaluation in the fields of criminal and juvenile justice. Her most recent research has been a national study of the manner in which police handle problem juveniles. Prior to this, Dr. Rovner-Pieczenik undertook a national study of pretrial intervention strategies for adults and juveniles, reviewed programs for offenders sponsored by the Department of Labor, and designed a methodology for evaluating the quality of legal services provided by public defenders. Dr. Rovner-Pieczenik's most recent book is entitled, *Pretrial Intervention Strategies* (Lexington Books, 1976).